GLOBALIZATION

GLOBALIZATION

•

Manfred B. Steger

A BRIEF
INSIGHT

STERLING

New York / London
www.sterlingpublishing.com

STERLING and the distinctive Sterling logo are registered trademarks of
Sterling Publishing Co., Inc.

Library of Congress Cataloging-in-Publication Data Available

10 9 8 7 6 5 4 3 2 1

Published by Sterling Publishing Co., Inc.
387 Park Avenue South, New York, NY 10016

Published by arrangement with Oxford University Press, Inc.

© 2009 by Manfred B. Steger
Illustrated edition published in 2010 by Sterling Publishing Co., Inc.
Additional text © 2010 Sterling Publishing Co., Inc.

Distributed in Canada by Sterling Publishing
c/o Canadian Manda Group, 165 Dufferin Street
Toronto, Ontario, Canada M6K 3H6

Book design: The DesignWorks Group

Please see picture credits on page 179 for image copyright information.

Printed in China

Sterling ISBN 978-1-4027-6878-1

For information about custom editions, special sales, premium and corporate purchases, please contact
Sterling Special Sales Department at 800-805-5489 or specialsales@sterlingpublishing.com.

Frontispiece: The globe at Flushing Meadows–Corona Park, photographed on September 1, 2005.

CONTENTS

•

PREFACE TO THE
SECOND EDITION

•

IT IS A GRATIFYING EXPERIENCE to present readers with a new edition of this introduction to globalization that has been so well received—not only in the English-speaking world, but, as its translation record shows, around the globe. However, the necessary task of updating and expanding the 2003 edition has made it difficult to keep a book on such a complex topic as "globalization" short and accessible. This challenge becomes even more formidable in the case of a short introduction. The authors of the few existing short introductions to the subject have opted to discuss only one aspect of globalization—usually the emerging global economic system, its history, structure, and supposed benefits and failings. While helpful in explaining the intricacies of international trade policy, global financial markets, worldwide flows of goods, services, and labor, transnational corporations, offshore financial centers, foreign direct investment, and the new international economic institutions, such narrow accounts often leave the general reader with a shallow understanding of globalization as primarily an economic phenomenon mediated by new technologies.

To be sure, the discussion of economic matters must be a significant part of any comprehensive account of globalization, but the latter should not be conflated with the former. The present volume makes the case that globalization is best thought of as a multidimensional set of social processes that resists being confined to any single thematic framework. Indeed, the transformative powers of globalization reach deeply into the economic, political, cultural, technological, and ecological dimensions of contemporary social life.

In addition, globalization contains important *ideological* aspects in the form of politically charged narratives that put before the public a particular agenda of topics for discussion, questions to ask, and claims to make. The existence of these narratives shows that globalization is not merely an objective process, but also a plethora of metaphors and stories that define, describe, and analyze that very process. The social forces behind these competing accounts of globalization seek to endow this concept with norms, values, and meanings that not only legitimate and advance specific power interests, but also shape the personal and collective identities of billions of people. In order to shed light on these rhetorical maneuvers, any introduction to globalization ought to examine its ideological dimension. After all, it is mostly the question of whether globalization ought to be considered a "good" or a "bad" thing that has spawned heated debates in classrooms, in boardrooms, and on the streets.

The study of globalization extends beyond particular academic disciplines. Yet, the lack of a firm disciplinary home also contains great opportunities. Global studies has been slowly emerging as a new field of academic study that cuts across traditional disciplinary boundaries in the social sciences and humanities. This strong emphasis on transdisciplinarity requires students of global studies to familiarize themselves with vast literatures on related subjects that are usually studied in isolation from each other. The greatest challenge facing global studies lies, therefore, in connecting and synthesizing the various strands of knowledge in a way that does justice to the increasingly fluid and interdependent nature of our fast-changing, postmodern world. In short, global studies requires an approach broad enough to behold the "big picture." Such a transdisciplinary enterprise may well lead to the rehabilitation of the academic generalist whose prestige, for too long, has been overshadowed by the specialist.

Finally, let me add a word of clarification. Although the main purpose of this book is to provide its audience with a descriptive and explanatory account of the various dimensions of globalization, the careful reader will detect throughout a critical approach. This pertains especially to the nature and the effects of what I call "market globalism." But my skepticism should not be interpreted as a blanket rejection of either markets or globalization. In fact, I appreciate the role of markets in facilitating necessary material exchanges. I also believe that we should take comfort in the fact that the world is becoming a more interdependent place that enhances people's chances to acknowledge their common humanity across arbitrarily drawn political borders and cultural divides. I also welcome the global flow of ideas and commodities, as well as the rapid development of technology, provided that they go hand in hand with greater forms of freedom and equality for *all* people, especially those living in the global South. Such compassionate forms of globalization are more attuned to what is shaping up to be humanity's most daunting task in the twenty-first century: the protection and preservation of our planet. Thus, the brunt of my critique is not directed at globalization per se, but at particular manifestations and tendencies that strike me as falling short of the noble vision of a more just and compassionate global order.

It is a pleasant duty to record my debts of gratitude. I want to thank my colleagues and friends at the Globalism Research Centre and the Global Cities Institute at the Royal Melbourne Institute of Technology (RMIT University) for their wonderful support of my research agenda. I also salute the faculty of the Department of Political Science and the Globalization Research Center at the University of Hawaii-Manoa for their steady encouragement.

Special thanks are due to Dr. Erin Wilson, my indefatigable colleague and research assistant at RMIT University, for helping me to put together this edition. I also want to express my deep appreciation to numerous readers, reviewers, and audiences around the world, who, for over more than a decade, made insightful comments in response to my public lectures and publications on the subject of globalization. Franz J. Broswimmer, a dear friend and innovative social thinker, deserves special recognition for supplying me with valuable information on the ecological aspects of globalization. Andrea Keegan and James Thompson, my editors at Oxford University Press, have been shining examples of professionalism and competence. Finally, I want to thank my wife, Perle—as well as the Steger and Besserman families—for their love and support. Many people have contributed to improving the quality of this book; its remaining flaws are my own responsibility.

ABBREVIATIONS

·

ABC	American Broadcasting Company
AOL	America Online
APEC	Asia-Pacific Economic Cooperation
ASEAN	Association of Southeast Asian Nations
BBC	British Broadcasting Corporation
BCE	Before the common era
CE	Common era
CEO	Chief executive officer
CFCs	Chlorofluorocarbons
CITES	Convention on International Trade in Endangered Species of Wild Fauna and Flora
CNN	Cable News Network
CNBC	Consumer News and Business Channel
EU	European Union
FTAA	Free Trade Area of the Americas
G8	Group of Eight
GATT	General Agreement on Tariffs and Trade
GDP	Gross domestic product
GNP	Gross national product

INGO	International nongovernmental organization
IMF	International Monetary Fund
MAI	Multilateral Agreement on Investment
MERCOSUR	Mercado Común del Sur (Southern Common Market)
MTV	Music Television
NAFTA	North American Free Trade Agreement
NATO	North Atlantic Treaty Organization
NGO	Nongovernmental organization
OECD	Organization for Economic Cooperation and Development
OPEC	Organization of Petroleum Exporting Countries
TNCs	Transnational Corporations
UN	United Nations
UNESCO	United Nations Educational, Scientific and Cultural Organization
WEF	World Economic Forum
WSF	World Social Forum
WTO	World Trade Organization

ONE

Globalization: A Contested Concept

●

Although the term *globalization* can be traced back to the early 1960s, it was not until a quarter of a century later that it took the public consciousness by storm. *Globalization* surfaced as *the* buzzword of the "Roaring Nineties" because it best captured the increasingly interdependent nature of social life on our planet. At the end of the opening decade of the twenty-first century, there were millions of references to globalization in both virtual and printed space. Unfortunately, however, early best sellers on the subject—Samuel Huntington's *The Clash of Civilizations*, Benjamin Barber's *Jihad Versus McWorld*, or Thomas Friedman's *The Lexus and the Olive Tree*—had left their readers with the simplistic impression that globalization was the inevitable process of a universalizing Western

Global economic, political, cultural, and environmental interconnections—many of which are made through advanced technologies such as this telecommunications satellite—make many of the world's current borders irrelevant and contribute to the social processes that lead to the phenomenon we know as globalization.

civilization battling the parochial forces of nationalism, localism, and tribalism. This influential assumption deepened further in the wake of the 9/11 attacks and the ensuing Global War on Terror spearheaded by an "American Empire" of worldwide reach. As a result of this rigid dichotomy that pitted the universal against the particular and the global against the local, many people had trouble recognizing the myriad ties binding religious-traditionalist fundamentalisms to the secular postmodernity of the global age.

As an illustration of this narrow perspective, let me introduce a bright history major from one of my global studies courses. "I understand that 'globalization' is a contested concept that refers to the shrinkage of time and space," she quipped, "but how can you say that religious fanatics who denounce modernity and secularism from a mountain cave somewhere in the Middle East perfectly capture the complex dynamics of globalization? Don't these terrible acts of terrorism suggest the opposite, namely, the growth of reactionary forces that undermine globalization?" Obviously, the student was referring to Saudi-born Al-Qaeda leader Osama bin Laden and his associates, whose videotaped statements condemning the activities of "infidel crusaders and Zionists" were the steady diet of worldwide broadcasts in the years following the 9/11 attacks.

To be fair, however, I could not help but be struck by the sense of intellectual urgency that fueled my student's question. It showed that globalization in all its dimensions remains an elusive concept without real-life examples capable of breathing shape, color, and sound into a vague term that continues to dominate the twenty-first-century media landscape. Hence, before delving into necessary matters of definition and analytical clarification, we ought to approach our subject in less abstract fashion. Let's begin our journey with a careful examination of the aforementioned videotapes. It will soon become fairly obvious why a deconstruction of those images provides important clues to the nature and dynamics of the phenomenon we have come to call "globalization."

Deconstructing Osama bin Laden

The most infamous of the bin Laden tapes was broadcast worldwide on October 7, 2001, less than a month after the collapse of the Twin Towers in lower Manhattan. The recording bears no date, but experts have estimated that it was made about two weeks before it was broadcast. The timing of its release appears to have been carefully planned so as to achieve the maximum effect on the day the United States commenced its bombing campaign against the Taliban and Al-Qaeda ("The Base") forces in Afghanistan. Although Osama bin Laden and his top lieutenants were then hiding in a remote region of the country, they obviously possessed the hi-tech equipment needed to record the statement. Moreover, Al-Qaeda members clearly enjoyed immediate access to sophisticated information and telecommunication networks that kept them informed—in real time—of relevant international developments. Bin Laden may have denounced the international "crusaders" with great conviction, but the smooth operation of his entire organization was entirely dependent on information and communication technology developed in the globalizing decades of the waning twentieth century.

To further illustrate this apparent contradiction, consider the complex chain of global interdependencies that must have existed in order for bin Laden's message to be heard and seen by countless TV viewers around the world. After making its way from the secluded mountains of eastern Afghanistan to the capital city of Kabul, the videotape was dropped off by an unknown courier outside the local office of Al-Jazeera,

Perfectly capturing the complex dynamics of globalization, Al-Qaeda leader Osama bin Laden addresses a global audience on October 7, 2001.

a Qatar-based television company. This network had been launched only five years earlier as a state-financed, Arabic-language news and current affairs channel that offered limited programming. Before the founding of Al-Jazeera, cutting-edge TV journalism—such as free-ranging public affairs interviews and talk shows with call-in audiences—simply did not exist in the Arab world. Within only three years, however, Al-Jazeera was offering its Middle Eastern audience a dizzying array of programs, transmitted around the clock by powerful satellites put into orbit by European rockets and American space shuttles.

Indeed, the network's market share increased even further as a result of the dramatic reduction in the price and size of satellite dishes. Suddenly, such technologies became affordable, even for low-income consumers.

By the turn of the century, Al-Jazeera broadcasts could be watched around the clock on all five continents.

In 2001, the company further intensified its global reach when its chief executives signed a lucrative cooperation agreement with CNN, the leading news network owned by the giant multinational corporation AOL-Time Warner. A few months later, when the world's attention shifted to the war in Afghanistan, Al-Jazeera had already positioned itself as a truly global player, powerful enough to rent equipment to such prominent news providers as Reuters and ABC, sell satellite time to the Associated Press and BBC, and design an innovative Arabic-language business news channel together with its other American network partner, CNBC.

Unhampered by national borders and geographical obstacles, cooperation among these sprawling news networks had become so efficient that CNN acquired and broadcast a copy of the Osama bin Laden tape only a few hours after it had been delivered to the Al-Jazeera office in Kabul. Caught off guard by the incredible speed of today's information exchange, the Bush administration asked the Qatari government to "rein in Al-Jazeera," claiming that the swift airing of the bin Laden tape without prior consultation was contributing to the rise of anti-American sentiments in the Arab world and thus threatened to undermine the US war effort. However, not only was the perceived "damage" already done, but segments of the tape—including the full text of bin Laden's statement—could be viewed online by anyone with access to a computer and a modem. The Al-Jazeera Web site quickly attracted an international audience as its daily hit count skyrocketed to over seven million.

There can be no doubt that it was the existence of this chain of global interconnections that made possible the instant broadcast of bin Laden's speech to a global audience. At the same time, however, it must be emphasized that even those voices that oppose modernity cannot extricate themselves from the very process of globalization they so decry. In order to spread their message and recruit new sympathizers, apparent "antiglobalizers" must utilize the tools provided by globalization. This obvious truth was visible even in bin Laden's personal appearance. The tape shows that he was wearing contemporary military fatigues over traditional Arab garments. In other words, his dress reflects the contemporary processes of fragmentation and cross-fertilization that global studies scholars call "hybridization"—the mixing of different cultural forms and styles facilitated by global economic and cultural exchanges. In fact, the pale colors of bin Laden's mottled combat dress betrayed its Russian origins, suggesting that

The rapid growth of Qatar-based television network Al-Jazeera, whose headquarters are shown in this 2007 photograph, was supported in part by technological advances achieved by nations far from its home base's borders. The network's ability to avail itself of these technological breakthroughs enabled the almost immediate worldwide dissemination of bin Laden's video message.

he wore the jacket as a symbolic reminder of the fierce guerrilla war waged by him and other Islamic militants against the Soviet occupation forces in Afghanistan during the 1980s.

His ever-present AK-47 Kalashnikov, too, was probably made in Russia, although dozens of gun factories around the world have been building this popular assault rifle for over forty years. By the mid-1990s, more than seventy million Kalashnikovs had been manufactured in Russia and abroad. At least fifty national armies include such rifles in their arsenal, making Kalashnikovs truly weapons of global choice. Thus, bin Laden's AK-47 could have come from anywhere in the world. However, given the astonishing globalization of organized crime during the last two decades, it is quite conceivable that bin Laden's rifle was part of an illegal arms deal hatched and executed by such powerful international criminal organizations as Al-Qaeda and the Russian Mafia. It is also possible that the rifle arrived in Afghanistan by means of an underground arms trade similar to the one that surfaced in May 1996, when police in San Francisco seized two thousand illegally imported AK-47s manufactured in China.

A close look at bin Laden's right wrist reveals yet another clue to the powerful dynamics of globalization. As he directs his words of contempt for the United States and its allies at his handheld microphone, his retreating sleeve exposes a stylish sports watch. Journalists who noticed this expensive accessory have speculated about its origins. The emerging consensus points to a Timex product. However, given that Timex watches are as American as apple pie, it seems rather ironic that the Al-Qaeda leader should have chosen this particular chronometer. After all, Timex Corporation, originally the Waterbury Clock Company, was founded in the 1850s in Connecticut's Naugatuck Valley, known throughout the

US Attorney Michael Yamaguchi is shown speaking at a news conference in San Francisco after the seizure of two thousand smuggled AK-47s.

nineteenth century as the "Switzerland of America." Today, Timex has gone multinational, maintaining close relations to affiliated businesses and sales offices in sixty-five countries. It employs seventy-five hundred employees, located on four continents. Thousands of workers—mostly from low-wage countries in the global South—constitute the driving force behind the corporation's global production process.

Our brief deconstruction of some of the central images on the videotape makes it easier to understand why the seemingly anachronistic images of an "antiglobalist" terrorist in front of an Afghan cave do, in fact, capture some essential dynamics of globalization. To be sure, in his subsequent taped appearances, Osama bin Laden presented himself more like a learned Muslim cleric than a holy warrior. In a September 2007 tape, he even went so far as to show off his neatly trimmed and dyed beard. But even this softened image of one of the world's most famous mujahideen ("holy warriors") doesn't change the overarching reality of intensifying global interdependence: the tensions between localism and globalism have reached unprecedented levels precisely because the links connecting them have been growing faster than at any time in history. The rise of worldwide terrorist organizations like Al-Qaeda represents but one of the many manifestations of globalization. Just as bin Laden's romantic ideology of a "pure Islam" is itself an articulation of the global imaginary, so has our global age, with its insatiable appetite for technology, mass-market commodities, and celebrities, indelibly shaped the violent backlash against globalization. Our deconstruction of Osama bin Laden has provided us with a real-life example of the intricate—and sometimes contradictory—social dynamics of globalization. We are now in a better position to tackle the rather demanding task of assembling a working definition of a contested concept that has proven to be notoriously hard to pin down.

Toward a Definition of Globalization

Globalization has been variously used in both popular and academic literature to describe a process, a condition, a system, a force, and an age. Given that these competing labels have very different meanings, their indiscriminate usage is often obscure and invites confusion. For example, a sloppy conflation of process and condition encourages circular definitions that explain little. The often repeated truism that "globalization [the process] leads to more globalization [the condition]" does not allow us to draw meaningful analytical distinctions between causes and effects.

Hence, I suggest that we adopt the term *globality* to signify a *social condition* characterized by tight global economic, political, cultural, and environmental interconnections and flows that make most of the currently existing borders and boundaries irrelevant. Yet, we should assume neither that globality is already upon us nor that it refers to a determinate endpoint that precludes any further development. Rather, this concept signifies a future social condition that, like all conditions, is destined to give way to new constellations. For example, it is conceivable that globality might eventually be transformed into something we might call "planetarity"—a new social condition brought about by the successful colonization of our solar system. Moreover, we could easily imagine different social manifestations of globality: one might be based primarily on values of individualism, competition, and laissez-faire capitalism, while another might draw on more communal and cooperative norms. These possible alternatives point to the fundamentally *indeterminate character* of globality.

The term *globalization* applies to a *set of social processes* that appear to transform our present social condition of weakening nationality into one of globality. At its core, then, globalization is about shifting forms of human contact. Indeed, any affirmation of globalization implies three assertions: first, we are slowly leaving behind the condition of modern nationality that gradually unfolded from the eighteenth century onward; second, we are moving toward the new condition of postmodern globality; and, third, we have not yet reached it. Indeed, like *modernization* and other verbal nouns that end in the suffix *-ization*, the term *globalization* suggests a sort of dynamism best captured by the notion of "development" or "unfolding" along discernible patterns. Such unfolding may occur quickly or slowly, but it always corresponds to the idea of change, and, therefore, denotes transformation.

Hence, academics exploring the dynamics of globalization are particularly keen on pursuing research questions related to the theme of social change. How does globalization occur? What is driving globalization? Is it one cause or a combination of factors? Is globalization a uniform or an uneven process? Is globalization a continuation of modernity or is it a radical break? How does globalization differ from previous social developments? Does globalization create new forms of inequality and hierarchy? Notice that the conceptualization of globalization as a dynamic process rather than as a static condition forces the researcher to pay close attention to shifting perceptions of time and space. This explains why many globalization scholars assign particular significance to historical analysis and the reconfiguration of social space. Indeed, the crucial insights of human geographers have played a major role in developing the field of global studies. Most important, these scholars point out that old geographical scales that distinguish sharply between *local*, *national*, *regional*, and *global* no longer work in a complex, networked world where these scales overlap and interpenetrate each other. Indeed, the best place to study the "global" is often the "local"—reflected, for example, in "global cities" like New York, London, Tokyo, and Shanghai.

Finally, let us adopt *global imaginary* as a concept referring to people's growing consciousness of belonging to a global community. This is not to say that national and local communal frameworks have lost their power to provide people with a meaningful sense of home and identity. But it would be a mistake to close one's eyes to the weakening of the national imaginary. As the global imaginary erupts with increasing frequency within and onto the national and local, it destabilizes and unsettles the conventional parameters of understanding within which people imagine their communal existence. As we shall see in later chapters, the rising global imaginary is also powerfully reflected in the current transformation of political ideologies—the ideas and beliefs that go into the articulation of concrete political agendas and programs.

To argue that globalization constitutes a set of social processes enveloped by the rising global imaginary and propelling us toward the condition of globality may eliminate the danger of circular definitions, but it gives us only one defining characteristic of the process: movement toward greater interdependence and integration. Such a general definition of globalization tells us little about its remaining qualities. In order to overcome this deficiency, let us identify additional qualities that make globalization different from other sets of social processes. Yet, whenever researchers raise the level of specificity in order to bring the phenomenon in question into sharper focus, they also heighten the danger of provoking scholarly disagreements over definitions. Our subject is no exception. One of the reasons why globalization remains a contested concept is because there exists no scholarly consensus on what kinds of social processes constitute its essence.

After all, globalization is an uneven process, meaning that people living in various parts of the world are affected very differently by this gigantic transformation of social structures and cultural zones. Hence, the social processes that make up globalization have been analyzed and explained by various commentators in different, often contradictory ways. Scholars not only hold different views with regard to proper definitions of globalization; they also disagree on its scale, causation, chronology, impact, trajectories, and policy outcomes. The ancient Buddhist parable of the blind scholars and their encounter with the

The ongoing academic quarrel over the definition of *globalization* is a postmodern version of the parable of the blind monks and the elephant, in which each man reaches a different conclusion based on which part of the elephant he has examined. The parable is illustrated here in an ukiyo-e color woodcut by Japanese artist Itchō Hanabusa (1652–1724).

elephant helps to illustrate the academic controversy over the nature and various dimensions of globalization.

Since the blind scholars did not know what the elephant looked like, they resolved to obtain a mental picture, and thus the knowledge they desired, by touching the animal. Feeling its trunk, one blind man argued that the elephant was like a lively snake. Another man, rubbing along its enormous leg, likened the animal to a rough column of massive proportions. The third person took hold of its tail and insisted that the elephant resembled a large, flexible brush. The fourth man felt its sharp tusks and declared it to be like a great spear. Each of the blind scholars held firmly to his own idea of what constituted an elephant. Since their scholarly reputation was riding on the veracity of their respective findings, the blind men eventually ended up arguing over the true nature of the elephant.

The ongoing academic quarrel over which dimension contains the essence of globalization represents a postmodern version of the parable of the blind men and the elephant. Even those few remaining scholars who still think of globalization as a singular process clash with each other over which aspect of social life constitutes its primary domain. Some global studies experts argue that economic processes lie at the core of globalization. Others privilege political, cultural, or ideological aspects. Still others point to environmental processes as the essence of globalization. Like the blind men in the parable, each globalization researcher is partly right by correctly identifying *one* important dimension of the phenomenon in question. However, their collective mistake lies in their dogmatic attempts to reduce such a complex phenomenon as globalization to a single domain that corresponds to their own expertise. Surely, one of the central tasks for global studies as an emerging field must be to devise better ways for gauging the relative importance of each dimension without losing sight of the interconnected whole. Fortunately, more and more researchers have begun to heed this call for a genuine multidimensional approach to globalization that avoids pernicious reductionism.

Despite such differences of opinion, it is nonetheless possible to detect some thematic overlap in various scholarly attempts to identify the core qualities of globalization processes. Consider, for example, the five influential definitions of globalization (see box).

These definitions point to four additional qualities or characteristics at the core of the phenomenon. First, globalization involves the *creation* of new, and the *multiplication* of existing, social networks and activities that cut across traditional political, economic, cultural, and geographical boundaries. As we have seen in the case of Al-Jazeera, the creation of today's satellite-news corporations is made possible by

· · · · ·

FIVE INFLUENTIAL DEFINITIONS OF GLOBALIZATION

Globalization can thus be defined as the intensification of world-wide social relations which link distant localities in such a way that local happenings are shaped by events occurring many miles away and vice versa.

Anthony Giddens, Former Director of the London School of Economics

The concept of globalization reflects the sense of an immense enlargement of world communication, as well as of the horizon of a world market, both of which seem far more tangible and immediate than in earlier stages of modernity.

Fredric Jameson, Professor of Literature, Duke University

Globalization may be thought of as a process (or set of processes) which embodies a transformation in the spatial organization of social relations and transactionsóassessed in terms of their extensity, intensity, velocity and impactógenerating transcontinental or interregional flows and networks of activity, interaction, and the exercise of power.

David Held, Professor of Political Science, London School of Economics

Globalization as a concept refers both to the compression of the world and the intensification of consciousness of the world as a whole.

Roland Robertson, Professor of Sociology,
University of Aberdeen, Scotland

Globalization compresses the time and space aspects of social relations.

James Mittelman, Professor of International Relations,
American University, Washington

· · · · ·

One of the qualities of most definitions of *globalization* is reflected in the expansion and stretching of social relations, activities, and interdependencies. Gigantic shopping malls, such as this one in Jakarta, Indonesia, which houses French (Vuitton), Italian (Bulgari), and American (Nautica) brands among others, offer commodities from all regions of the world.

the combination of professional networking, technological innovation, and political decisions that permit the emergence of new social orders that transcend nationally based arrangements.

The second quality of globalization is reflected in the *expansion* and the *stretching* of social relations, activities, and interdependencies.

Today's financial markets reach around the globe, and electronic trading occurs around the clock. Gigantic and virtually identical shopping malls have emerged on all continents, offering those consumers who can afford commodities from all regions of the world—including products whose various components were manufactured in different countries. This process of social stretching applies to the Al-Qaeda terrorist network as well as to less sinister associations such as nongovernmental organizations, commercial enterprises, social clubs, and countless regional and global institutions and associations: the United Nations, the European Union, the Association of Southeast Asian Nations, the Organization of African Unity, Doctors Without Borders, the World Social Forum, or Google, to name but a few.

Third, globalization involves the *intensification* and *acceleration* of social exchanges and activities. As the Spanish sociologist Manuel Castells has pointed out, the creation of a global "network society" required a technological revolution—one that has been powered chiefly by the rapid development of new information and transportation technologies. Proceeding at breakneck speed, these innovations are reshaping the social landscape of human life. The Internet relays distant information in real time, and satellites provide consumers with instant pictures of remote events. The intensification of worldwide social relations means that local happenings are shaped by events occurring far away, and vice versa. In other words, the seemingly opposing processes of globalization and localization actually imply each other. Rather than sitting at the base and the top of conventional geographical hierarchies, the local and global intermingle messily with the national and regional in new horizontal scales.

Fourth, as we emphasized in our discussion of the global imaginary, globalization processes do not occur merely on an objective, material level but also involve the subjective plane of human consciousness. The compression of the world into a single place increasingly makes global the frame of reference for human thought and action. Hence, globalization involves both the macrostructures of community and the microstructures of personhood. It extends deep into the core of the self and its dispositions, facilitating the creation of new individual and collective identities nurtured by the intensifying relations between the individual and the globe.

It seems that we have succinctly identified some of the core qualities of globalization. Compressing them into a single sentence yields the following very short definition of globalization:

> Globalization refers to the expansion and intensification of social relations and consciousness across world-time and world-space.

Before we draw this chapter to a close, let us consider some objections raised by those scholars who belong to the camp of the "globalization skeptics." Their objections range from the accusation that fashionable "globalization talk" amounts to little more than "globaloney" to less radical suggestions that globalization is a much more limited and uneven process than the sweeping arguments of the so-called hyperglobalizers would have us believe. In many ways, the most radical globalization skeptics resemble the blind scholar who, occupying the empty space between the elephant's front and hind legs, groped in vain for a part of the elephant. Finding none, he accused his colleagues of making up fantastic stories about nonexistent things, asserting that there were no such animals as "elephants" at all. Since evidence pointing to the rapid intensification of worldwide social relations has been mounting in the 2000s, I will resist delving into a detailed refutation of those few remaining skeptics who deny the existence of globalization altogether.

Still, globalization skeptics performed the valuable service of forcing global studies scholars to hone their arguments. One of the most challenging questions posed by globalization skeptics is a historical one: is globalization a modern phenomenon? Some critics would respond to this question in the negative, insisting that the concept of globalization has been used in a historically imprecise manner. In a nutshell, this thoughtful group of skeptics contends that even a cursory look at history suggests that there is not much that is "new" about contemporary globalization. Hence, before we explore in some detail the main dimensions of globalization in subsequent chapters of this book, I suggest we give this weighty historical argument a fair hearing. Indeed, such a critical investigation of globalization's alleged novelty is closely related to yet another question hotly debated in global studies. What does a proper chronology and historical periodization of globalization look like? Let us turn to Chapter 2 to seek answers to these questions.

TWO

Globalization and History: Is Globalization a New Phenomenon?

●

IF WE ASKED AN ORDINARY PERSON on the busy streets of global cities like London, New York, or Singapore about the essence of globalization, the answer would probably involve some reference to growing forms of political and economic interdependence fuelled by "new technologies" like personal computers, the Internet, cellular phones, pagers, personal digital assistants like the popular Black-Berry, digital cameras, high-definition television, satellites, jet planes, space shuttles, and supertankers. As subsequent chapters will show,

The enhancement of worldwide interdependence and the general growth of awareness of deepening global connections are gradual processes with deep historical roots. The invention of the wheel around 3000 BCE made possible the faster and more efficient transport of goods and people, and the later standardization of cart axles and the roads they traveled in premodern China allowed Chinese merchants to make precise calculations regarding imported and exported goods. This hand-colored woodcut shows trade caravans on the Silk Road, which linked the Chinese and Roman empires.

however, technology provides only a partial explanation for the latest wave of globalization. Yet, it would be foolish to deny that these new innovations have played a crucial role in the expansion and intensification of social relations and consciousness across world-time and world-space. The Internet, in particular, has assumed a pivotal function in facilitating globalization through the creation of the World Wide Web that connects billions of individuals, civil society associations, and governments. Since most of these technologies have been around for less than three decades, it seems to make sense to agree with those commentators who claim that globalization is, indeed, a relatively new phenomenon.

At the same time, however, the definition of globalization we arrived at in the previous chapter stresses the dynamic nature of the phenomenon. The enhancement of worldwide interdependence and the rise of the global imaginary are gradual processes with deep historical roots. The engineers who developed laptop computers and supersonic jet planes stand on the shoulders of earlier innovators who created the steam engine, the cotton gin, the telegraph, the phonograph, the telephone, the typewriter, the internal-combustion engine, and electrical appliances. These products, in turn, owe their existence to much earlier technological inventions such as the telescope, the compass, water wheels, windmills, gunpowder, the printing press, and ocean-going ships. In order to acknowledge the full historical record, we might reach back even further to such momentous technological and social achievements as the production of paper, the development of writing, the invention of the wheel, the domestication of wild plants and animals, the emergence of language, and, finally, the slow outward migration of our African ancestors at the dawn of human evolution.

Globalization is a dynamic phenomenon, and the engineers who developed laptop computers and supersonic jet planes are indebted to the innovators who came before them, who created the steam engine, the cotton gin, and the phonograph, for example. American inventor Thomas Alva Edison is shown here in a ca. 1877 photograph with an early version of his phonograph.

Thus, the answer to the question of whether globalization constitutes a new phenomenon depends upon how far we are willing to extend the chain of causation that resulted in those recent technologies and social arrangements that most people have come to associate with this fashionable buzzword. Some scholars consciously limit the historical scope of globalization to the post-1989 era or the last four decades of postindustrialism in order to capture its contemporary features. Others are willing to extend this timeframe to include the groundbreaking developments of the nineteenth century. Still others argue that globalization really represents the continuation and extension of complex processes that began with the emergence of modernity and the capitalist world system some five centuries ago. And a few remaining researchers refuse to confine globalization to time periods measured in mere decades or centuries. Rather, they suggest that these processes have been unfolding for millennia.

No doubt, each of these contending perspectives contains important insights. As we will see in subsequent chapters, the advocates of the first approach have marshaled impressive evidence for their view that the dramatic expansion and acceleration of global exchanges since the 1970s and 1980s represent a quantum leap in the history of globalization. The proponents of the second view correctly emphasize the tight connection between contemporary forms of globalization and the explosion of technology known as the Industrial Revolution. The representatives of the third perspective rightly point to the significance of the time-space compression that occurred in the sixteenth century when Eurasia, Africa, and the Americas first became connected by enduring trade routes. Finally, the advocates of the fourth approach advance a rather sensible argument when they insist that any truly comprehensive account of globalization falls short without the incorporation of ancient developments and enduring dynamics into our planetary history.

While the short chronology outlined below is necessarily fragmentary and general, it nonetheless highlights the fact that globalization is a long-term phenomenon. This brief sketch identifies five historical periods that are separated from each other by significant accelerations in the pace of social exchanges as well as a widening of their geographical scope. Thus, we could say that globalization is a long-term process that, over many centuries, has crossed distinct qualitative thresholds. In this context, it is important to bear in mind that my chronology does not necessarily imply a linear unfolding of history, nor does it advocate a conventional Eurocentric perspective of world history. Full of unanticipated surprises, violent twists, sudden punctuations, and dramatic reversals, the history of globalization has involved all major regions and cultures of our planet.

The Prehistoric Period (10,000 BCE–3500 BCE)

Let us begin our brief historical sketch of globalization about twelve thousand years ago when small bands of hunters and gatherers reached the southern tip of South America. This event marked the end of the long process of settling all five continents that was begun by our hominid African ancestors more than one million years ago. Although some major island groups in the Pacific and the Atlantic were not inhabited until relatively recent times, the truly global dispersion of our species was finally achieved. The successful endeavor of the South American nomads rested on the migratory achievements of their Siberian ancestors who had crossed the Bering Strait into North America a thousand years earlier.

In this earliest phase of globalization, contact among thousands of hunter and gatherer bands spread all over the world was geographically limited and mostly coincidental. This fleeting mode of social interaction changed dramatically about ten thousand years ago when humans took the crucial step of producing their own food. As a result of several factors, including the natural occurrence of plants and animals suitable for domestication as well as continental differences in area and total population size, only certain regions located on or near the vast Eurasian landmass proved to be ideal for these growing agricultural settlements. These areas were located in the Fertile Crescent, north-central China, North Africa, northwestern India, and New Guinea. Over time, food surpluses achieved by these early farmers and herders

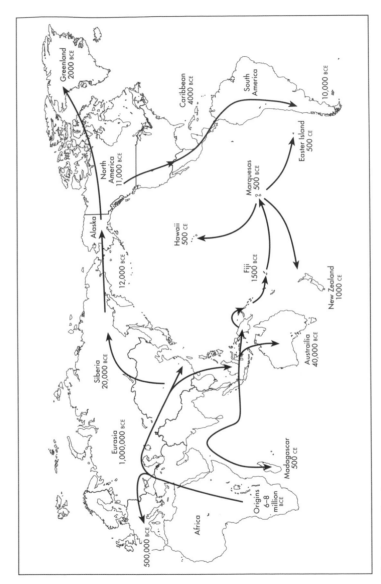

Early human migrations.

led to population increases, the establishment of permanent villages, and the construction of fortified towns.

Roving bands of nomads lost out to settled tribes, chiefdoms, and, ultimately, powerful states based on agricultural food production.

The decentralized, egalitarian nature of hunter and gatherer groups was replaced by centralized and highly stratified patriarchal social structures headed by chiefs and priests who were exempted from hard manual labor. Moreover, for the first time in human history, these farming societies were able to support two additional social classes whose members did not participate in food production. One group consisted of full-time craft specialists who directed their creative energies toward the invention of new technologies, such as powerful iron tools and beautiful ornaments made of precious metals, complex irrigation canals, sophisticated pottery and basketry, and monumental building structures. The other group was comprised of professional bureaucrats and soldiers who would later play a key role in the monopolization of the means of violence in the hands of the rulers, the precise accounting of food surpluses necessary for the growth and survival of the centralized state, the acquisition of new

The prehistoric period marked the first time societies were divided into classes and saw the development of powerful tools and sophisticated metal and pottery work. Still, globalization dynamics during this era were limited in scope and reach. This cord-marked amphora from about 4800 BCE was found in Shaanxi, China.

territory, the establishment of permanenttrade routes, and the systematic exploration of distant regions.

For the most part, however, globalization in the prehistoric period was severely limited. Advanced forms of technology capable of overcoming existing geographical and social obstacles were largely absent; thus, enduring long-distance interactions never materialized. It was only toward the end of this epoch that centrally administered forms of agriculture, religion, bureaucracy, and warfare slowly emerged as the key agents of intensifying modes of social exchange that would involve a growing number of societies in many regions of the world.

The Premodern Period (3500 BCE–1500 BCE)

The invention of writing in Mesopotamia, Egypt, and central China between 3500 and 2000 BCE roughly coincided with the invention of the wheel around 3000 BCE in southwest Asia. Marking the close of the prehistoric period, these monumental inventions amounted to one of those technological and social boosts that moved globalization to a new level. Thanks to the auspicious east-west orientation of Eurasia's major continental axis—a geographical feature that had already facilitated the rapid spread of crops and animals suitable for food production along the same latitudes—the diffusion of these new technologies to distant parts of the continent occurred within only a few centuries. The importance of these inventions for the strengthening of globalization processes should be obvious. Among other things, the wheel spurred crucial infrastructural innovations such as animal-drawn carts and permanent roads that allowed for the faster and more efficient transportation of people and goods. In addition to the spread of ideas and inventions, writing greatly facilitated the coordination of complex

The invention of writing in the premodern period aided the spread of ideas and inventions and facilitated the coordination of complex social activities, which encouraged the formation of large states. This stamping mold for the foundation bricks of the temple of the sun god Utu from about 1850 BCE is from the Sumerian civilization of southern Iraq.

social activities and thus encouraged large state formations. Of the sizable territorial units that arose during this period, only the Andes civilizations of South America managed to grow into the mighty Inca Empire without the benefits of either the wheel or the written word.

Thus the premodern period was the age of empires. As some states succeeded in establishing permanent rule over other states, the resulting vast territorial accumulations formed the basis of the Egyptian kingdoms, the Persian Empire, the Macedonian Empire, the American empires of the Aztecs and the Incas, the Roman Empire, the Indian empires, the Byzantine Empire, the Islamic caliphates, the Holy Roman Empire, the African empires of Ghana, Mali, and Songhay, and the Ottoman Empire. All of these empires fostered the multiplication and extension of long-distance communication and the exchange of culture, technology, commodities, and diseases. The most enduring and technologically advanced of these vast premodern conglomerates was undoubtedly the Chinese Empire. A closer look at its history reveals some of the early dynamics of globalization.

After centuries of warfare between several independent states, the Qin emperor's armies, in 221 BCE, finally unified large portions of northeast China. For the next seventeen hundred years, successive dynasties known as the Han, Sui, T'ang, Yuan, and Ming ruled an empire supported by vast bureaucracies that would extend its influence to such distant regions as tropical Southeast Asia, the Mediterranean, India, and East Africa. Dazzling artistry and brilliant philosophical achievements stimulated new discoveries in other fields of knowledge such as astronomy, mathematics, and chemistry. The long list of major technological innovations achieved in China during the premodern period include redesigned

The Chinese Empire was the most technologically advanced of the premodern conglomerates. This image, created in 1249, shows the stages of salt manufacture during the Sung dynasty (960–1280 CE).

ploughshares, hydraulic engineering, gunpowder, the tapping of natural gas, the compass, mechanical clocks, paper, printing, lavishly embroidered silk fabrics, and sophisticated metalworking techniques. The construction of vast irrigation systems consisting of hundreds of small canals enhanced the region's agricultural productivity while at the same time providing for one of the best river transport systems in the world. The codification of law and the fixing of weights, measures, and values of coinage fostered the expansion of trade and markets. The standardization of the size of cart axles and the roads they traveled on allowed Chinese merchants for the first time to make precise calculations as to the desired quantities of imported and exported goods.

The most extensive of these trade routes was the Silk Road. It linked the Chinese and the Roman empires, with Parthian traders serving as skilled intermediaries. Even thirteen hundred years after the Silk Road first reached the Italian peninsula, in 50 BCE, a truly multicultural group of Eurasian and African globetrotters—including the famous Moroccan merchant Ibn Battuta and his Venetian counterparts in the Marco Polo family—relied on this great Eurasian land route to reach the splendid imperial court of the Mongol Khans in Beijing.

By the fifteenth century CE, enormous Chinese fleets consisting of hundreds of four-hundred-foot-long oceangoing ships were crossing the Indian Ocean and establishing short-lived trade outposts on the east coast of Africa. However, a few decades later, the rulers of the Chinese Empire's series of fateful political decisions to turn inward halted overseas navigation and mandated a retreat from further technological development. Thus, the rulers cut short their empire's incipient industrial revolution, a development that allowed much smaller European states to emerge as the primary historical agents behind the intensification of globalization.

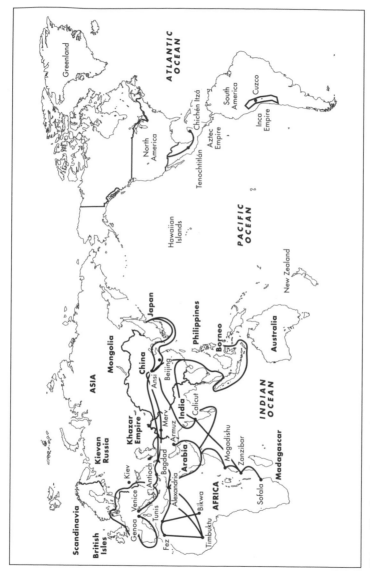

Major world trade networks, 1000–1450.

Toward the end of the premodern period, then, the existing global trade network consisted of several interlocking trade circuits that connected the most populous regions of Eurasia and northeastern Africa. Although both the Australian and the American continents still remained separate from this expanding web of economic, political, and cultural interdependence, the empires of the Aztecs and Incas had also succeeded in developing major trade networks in their own hemisphere.

The existence of these sprawling networks of economic and cultural exchange triggered massive waves of migration, which, in turn, led to further population increase and the rapid growth of urban centers. In the resulting cultural clashes, religions with only local significance were transformed into the major "world religions" we know today as Judaism, Christianity, Islam, Hinduism, and Buddhism. But higher population density and more intense social interaction over greater distances also facilitated the spread of new infectious diseases like the bubonic plague. The enormous plague epidemic of the mid-fourteenth century, for example, killed up to one-third of the respective populations of China, the Middle East, and Europe. However, these unwelcome by-products of unfolding globalization processes did not reach their most horrific manifestation until the fateful sixteenth-century collision of the "old" and "new" worlds, when the nasty germs of European invaders killed an estimated eighteen million Native Americans.

The Early Modern Period (1500–1750)

The term *modernity* has become associated with the eighteenth-century European Enlightenment project of developing objective science, achieving a universal form of morality and law, and liberating rational modes of thought and social organization from the perceived irrationalities

European powers during the early modern period failed to penetrate the interior of Africa and Asia and so turned their attention to westward expansion; their efforts were aided in part by improved navigational techniques. This map, from 1581, and picturing English navigator and buccaneer Sir Francis Drake, was made after Drake had completed his three-year circumnavigation of the world.

of myth, religion, and political tyranny. The label "early modern," then, refers to the period between the Enlightenment and the Renaissance. During these two centuries, Europe and its social practices served as the primary catalyst for globalization. Having contributed little to technology and other civilizational achievements before about 1000 CE, Europeans northwest of the Alps greatly benefited from the diffusion

of technological innovations originating in Islamic and Chinese cultural spheres. Despite the weakened political influence of China and the noticeable ecological decline of the Fertile Crescent (Mesopotamia) some five hundred years later, European powers failed to penetrate into the interior of Africa and Asia.

Instead, they turned their expansionistic desires westward, searching for a new, profitable sea route to India. Their efforts were aided by such innovations as mechanized printing, sophisticated wind and water mills, extensive postal systems, revised maritime technologies, and advanced navigation techniques. Add the enormous impact of the Reformation that reduced the power of the Catholic Church and helped spread related "liberal" ideas of individualism and limited government, and we have identified the main forces behind the qualitative leap that greatly intensified demographic, cultural, ecological, and economic flows between Europe, Africa, and the Americas.

Of course, the rise of European metropolitan centers and their affiliated merchant classes represented another important factor responsible for strengthening globalization tendencies during the early modern period. Embodying the new values of individualism and unlimited material accumulation, European economic entrepreneurs laid the foundation of what later scholars would call the "capitalist world system."

The monarchs of Spain, Portugal, the Netherlands, France, and England all put significant resources toward the exploration of new worlds. This chromolithograph published in 1893 shows Christopher Columbus at the court of Barcelona, before Queen Isabella and King Ferdinand of Spain.

However, these fledgling capitalists could not have achieved the global expansion of their commercial enterprises without substantial support from their respective governments. The monarchs of Spain, Portugal, the Netherlands, France, and England all put significant resources into the exploration of new worlds and the construction of new inter-regional markets that benefited them much more than their exotic "trading partners." By the early 1600s, national joint-stock companies like the Dutch and British East India companies were founded for the express purpose of setting up profitable overseas trade posts. As these innovative corporations grew in size and stature, they acquired the power to regulate most intercontinental economic transactions, in

Military and political alliances underwent continuous modification because of protracted religious wars. The Thirty Years War, which was fought from 1618 to 1648, began primarily as a conflict between Protestants and Catholics. This color copperplate depicts the siege of Stralsund, Germany, which lasted eleven weeks during the summer of 1628.

the process implementing social institutions and cultural practices that enabled later colonial governments to place these foreign regions under direct political rule. Related developments, such as the Atlantic slave trade and forced population transfers within the Americas, resulted in the suffering and death of millions of non-Europeans while greatly benefiting white immigrants and their home countries.

To be sure, religious warfare within Europe also created its share of dislocation and displacement for Caucasian populations. Moreover, as a result of these protracted armed conflicts, military alliances and political arrangements underwent continuous modification. Ultimately evolving from the Westphalian states system, the sovereign, territorial nation-state had emerged by 1648 as the modern container of social life. As the early modern period drew to a close, interdependencies among nation-states were multiplying as well as increasing in density.

The Modern Period (1750–1970)

By the late eighteenth century, Australia and the Pacific islands were slowly incorporated into the European-dominated network of political, economic, and cultural exchange. Increasingly confronted with stories of the "distant" and images of countless "others," Europeans and their descendants on other continents took it upon themselves to assume the role of the world's guardians of universal law and morality. In spite of their persistent claims to civilizational leadership, however, they remained strangely oblivious to their racist practices and the appalling conditions of inequality that existed both within their own societies and between the West and the "rest." Fed by a steady stream of materials and resources that originated mostly in other regions of the world, Western capitalist enterprises gained in stature. Daring to resist powerful governmental controls, economic entrepreneurs and their academic counterparts began to spread a philosophy of individualism and rational self-interest that glorified the virtues of an idealized capitalist system supposedly based upon the providential workings of the free market and its "invisible hand."

Written in 1847 by the German political radicals Karl Marx and Friedrich Engels, the boxed passage, taken from their famous *Communist Manifesto*, captures the qualitative shift in social relations that pushed globalization to a new level in the modern period.

> The discovery of America prepared the way for mighty industry and its creation of a truly global market. The latter greatly expanded trade, navigation, and communication by land. These developments, in turn, caused the further expansion of industry. The growth of industry, trade, navigation, and railroads also went hand in hand with the rise of the bourgeoisie and capital which pushed to the background the old social classes of the Middle Ages. . . . Chased around the globe by its burning desire for ever-expanding markets for its products, the bourgeoisie has no choice but to settle everywhere; cultivate everywhere; establish connections everywhere. . . . Rapidly improving the instruments of production, the bourgeoisie utilizes the incessantly easing modes of communication to pull all nations into civilization—even the most barbarian ones. . . . In a nutshell, it creates the world in its own image. (Translated by the author)

Indeed, the volume of world trade increased dramatically between 1850 and 1914. Guided by the activities of multinational banks, capital and goods flowed across the borders relatively freely as the sterling-based gold standard made possible the worldwide circulation of leading national currencies like the British pound and the Dutch guilder. Eager to acquire their own independent resource bases, most European nation-states subjected large portions of the global South to direct colonial rule. On the eve of the First World War, merchandise trade measured as a percentage of gross national output totaled almost 12 percent for the industrialized countries, a level unmatched until the 1970s. Global pricing systems facilitated trade in important commodities like grains, cotton, and various metals. Brand-name packaged goods like Coca-Cola drinks, Campbell soups, Singer sewing machines, and Remington typewriters made their first appearance. In order to raise the global visibility of these corporations, international advertising agencies launched the first full-blown transborder commercial promotion campaigns.

As Marx and Engels noted, however, the rise of the European bourgeoisie and the related intensification of global interconnections would not have been possible without the nineteenth-century explosion of science and technology. To be sure, the maintenance of these new industrial regimes required new power sources such as electricity and petroleum. The largely unregulated use of these energy sources resulted in the annihilation of countless animal and plant species as well as the toxification of entire regions. On the upside, however, railways, mechanized shipping, and twentieth-century intercontinental air transport managed to overcome the last remaining geographical obstacles to the establishment of a genuine global infrastructure, while at the same time lowering transportation costs.

These innovations in transportation were complemented by the swift development of communication technologies. The telegraph

Between 1850 and 1914, the volume of world trade increased dramatically, and brands such as Singer sewing machines made their appearance on the world market. This Singer advertisement was created around 1892.

and its transatlantic reach after 1866 provided for instant information exchanges between the two hemispheres. Moreover, the telegraph set the stage for the telephone and wireless radio communication, prompting newly emerging communication corporations like AT&T to coin advertising slogans in celebration of a world "inextricably bound together." Finally, the twentieth-century arrival of mass circulation

Advances in communication technologies such as transatlantic telegraphy led the way to the advent of the telephone. This 1866 color lithograph celebrating "The Eighth Wonder of the World—The Atlantic Cable," shows Neptune with a trident in the foreground, with a lion (Great Britain) holding one end of the Atlantic cable, and an eagle (the United States) holding the other. The inventor, Cyrus Field, is shown at top center.

newspapers and magazines, film, and television further enhanced a growing consciousness of a rapidly shrinking world.

The modern period also witnessed an unprecedented population explosion. Having increased only modestly from about 300 million at the time of the birth of Christ to 760 million in 1750, the world's population reached 3.7 billion in 1970. Enormous waves of migration intensified existing cultural exchanges and transformed traditional social patterns. Popular immigration countries like the United States of America, Canada, and Australia took advantage of this boost in productivity. By the early twentieth century, these countries entered the world stage as forces to be reckoned with. At the same time, however, they made significant efforts to control these large migratory flows, in the process inventing novel forms of bureaucratic control and developing new surveillance techniques designed to accumulate more information about nationals while keeping "undesirables" out.

When the accelerating process of industrialization sharpened existing disparities in wealth and well-being beyond bearable limits, many working people in the global North began to organize themselves politically in various labor movements and socialist parties. However, their idealistic calls for international class solidarity went largely unheeded. Instead, ideologies that translated the national imaginary into extreme political programs captured the imagination of millions of people around the world. There is no question that interstate rivalries intensified at the outset of the twentieth century as a result of mass migration, urbanization, colonial competition, and the excessive liberalization of world trade. The ensuing period of extreme nationalism culminated in two devastating world wars, a long global economic depression, and hostile measures to protect narrowly conceived political communities.

The end of the Second World War saw the explosion of two powerful atomic bombs that killed nearly two hundred thousand Japanese, most of them civilians. Nothing did more to convince people around the world of the linked fate of geographically and politically separated "nations." Indeed, the global imaginary found a horrifying expression in

Interstate rivalries heightened at the beginning of the twentieth century as a result of mass migration, urbanization, colonial competition, and the liberalization of world trade. This photograph from the early 1900s shows immigrants arriving at Ellis Island, New York. The island's peak year for immigration was 1907, when approximately 1.25 million immigrants were processed at the facility.

the Cold War acronym MAD (mutually assured destruction). A more positive result was the process of decolonization in the 1950s and 1960s that slowly revived global flows and international exchanges. The new "international system" of sovereign yet interdependent nation-states anchored in the charter of the United Nations raised the prospect of global democratic governance. However, such cosmopolitan hopes quickly faded as the Cold War divided the world for four long decades into two antagonistic spheres: a liberal-capitalist "First World" dominated by the United States, and an authoritarian-socialist "Second World" controlled by the Soviet Union. Both blocs sought to establish their political and ideological dominance in the "Third World." Indeed, superpower confrontations like the Cuban missile crisis raised the specter of a global conflict capable of destroying virtually all life on our planet.

The Contemporary Period (from 1970)

As we noted at the beginning of this chapter, the dramatic creation, expansion, and acceleration of worldwide interdependencies and global exchanges that have occurred since the early 1970s represent yet another quantum leap in the history of globalization. These dynamics received another boost with the collapse of Soviet-style communism and attempts to create a single global market. But what exactly is happening? Why does what is happening justify the creation of a buzzword that has not only captured the public imagination, but has also elicited such powerful conflicting emotional responses? Is contemporary globalization a "good" or a "bad" thing? Throughout this book we will consider possible answers to these crucial questions. In doing so, we will limit the application of the term *globalization* to the contemporary period while keeping in mind that the dynamic driving these processes actually started thousands of years ago.

Before we embark on this next stage of our journey, let us pause and recall an important point we made in Chapter 1. Globalization is not a single process but a set of processes that operate simultaneously and unevenly on several levels and in various dimensions. We could compare these interactions and interdependencies to an intricate tapestry of overlapping shapes and colors. Yet, just as an auto mechanic apprentice must turn off and disassemble the car engine in order to understand its operation, so must the student of globalization apply analytical distinctions in order to make sense of the web of global interdependencies. In ensuing chapters we will identify, explore, and assess patterns of globalization in each of its main domains—economic, political, cultural, ecological, and ideological—while keeping in mind its operation as an interacting whole. Although we will study the various dimensions of globalization in isolation, we will resist the temptation to reduce globalization to a single aspect. Thus will we avoid the blunder that kept the blind men from appreciating the multidimensional nature of the elephant.

THREE

The Economic Dimension of Globalization

●

AT THE BEGINNING OF THE previous chapter we noted that new forms of technology are one of the hallmarks of contemporary globalization. Indeed, technological progress of the magnitude seen in the last three decades is a good indicator for the occurrence of profound social transformations centered on the market. Changes in the way in which people undertake economic production and organize the exchange of commodities represent one obvious aspect of the great transformation of our age. Economic globalization refers to the intensification and stretching of economic interrelations across the globe. Gigantic flows of capital and technology have stimulated trade in goods and services. Markets have

Economic globalization **refers** to the intensification and stretching of economic interrelations across the globe. The trading floor of the New York Stock Exchange is pictured here in a photograph taken on January 23, 2008.

extended their reach around the world, in the process creating new linkages among national economies. Huge transnational corporations, powerful international economic institutions, and large regional trading systems have emerged as the major building blocks of the twenty-first century's global economic order.

The Emergence of the Global Economic Order

Contemporary economic globalization can be traced back to the gradual emergence of a new international economic order assembled at an economic conference held toward the end of the Second World War in the sleepy New England town of Bretton Woods. Under the leadership of the United States of America and Great Britain, the major economic powers of the global North reversed their economic policies of the interwar period (1918–39), which, for example, introduced high tariffs on imported goods to protect the national economy. In addition to arriving at a firm commitment to expand international trade, the participants in the conference also agreed to establish binding rules on international economic activities. Moreover, they resolved to create a more stable money exchange system in which the value of each country's currency was pegged to a fixed gold value of the US dollar. Within these prescribed limits, individual nations were free to control the permeability of their borders. This allowed states to set their own political and economic agendas.

Bretton Woods also set the institutional foundations for the establishment of three new international economic organizations. The International Monetary Fund was created to administer the international monetary system. The International Bank for Reconstruction and Development, later known as the World Bank, was initially designed to provide loans for Europe's postwar reconstruction. During the 1950s, however, its

Contemporary economic globalization can be traced back to the Bretton Woods Conference, held toward the end of World War II. Participants arrived at a firm commitment to expand international trade and agreed to establish binding rules on international economic activities. This photograph, taken on July 4, 1944, shows conferees meeting at the Mount Washington Hotel in Bretton Woods, New Hampshire.

purpose was expanded to fund various industrial projects in developing countries around the world. Finally, the General Agreement on Tariffs and Trade was established in 1947 as a global trade organization charged with fashioning and enforcing multilateral trade agreements. In 1995, the World Trade Organization was founded as the successor organization to GATT. In the 1990s, the WTO became the focal point of intense public controversy over the design and the effects of economic globalization.

In operation for almost three decades, the Bretton Woods regime contributed greatly to the establishment of what some observers have called the "golden age of controlled capitalism." National governments

controlled money flows into and out of their territories. High taxation rates on wealthy individuals and profitable corporations led to the
expansion of the welfare state. Rising wages and increased social services in the wealthy countries of the global North appeared to offer
workers entry into the "middle class." By the early 1970s, however, the
Bretton Woods system collapsed. Its demise strengthened a new global
economic order based on expanding free markets. What happened?

In response to profound political changes in the world that were
undermining the economic competitiveness of US-based industries,
President Richard Nixon abandoned the gold-based fixed rate system
in 1971. The ensuing decade was characterized by global economic
instability in the form of high inflation, low economic growth, high
unemployment, public sector deficits, and two unprecedented energy
crises due to OPEC's ability to control a large part of the world's
oil supply. Political forces in the global North most closely identified
with the model of controlled capitalism suffered a series of spectacular election defeats at the hands of conservative political parties who
advocated a "neoliberal" approach to economic and social policy.

· · · · ·

NEOLIBERALISM

Neoliberalism is rooted in the classical liberal ideals of Adam
Smith (1723–90) and David Ricardo (1772–1823), both of whom
viewed the market as a self-regulating mechanism tending toward
equilibrium of supply and demand, thus securing the most efficient allocation of resources. These British philosophers considered that any constraint on free competition would interfere with
the natural efficiency of market mechanisms, inevitably leading

to social stagnation, political corruption, and the creation of unresponsive state bureaucracies. They also advocated the elimination of tariffs on imports and other barriers to trade and capital flows between nations. British sociologist Herbert Spencer (1820–1903) added to this doctrine a twist of social Darwinism by arguing that free market economies constitute the most civilized form of human competition in which the "fittest" would naturally rise to the top.

Etching of Adam Smith by Cadell and Davies (1811), John Horsburgh (1828), or R. C. Bell (1872) after a 1787 portrait by James Tassie.

Illustration of David Ricardo (1888) from an engraving by Hodgets after a picture by T. Phillips, R. A.

· · · · ·

Yet, in the decades following the Second World War, even the most conservative political parties in Europe and the United States rejected those laissez-faire ideas and instead embraced a rather extensive version

Ronald Reagan and Margaret Thatcher's neoliberal revolution against Keynesianism was further legitimated by the fall of communism in the Soviet Union and Eastern Europe. The Berlin Wall, which had divided communist East Berlin from West Berlin since 1961, fell in November 1989. A portion of the wall, which was substantially demolished, although parts have been left standing as memorials, is shown here in front of the EU Parliament building in Brussels, Belgium.

of state interventionism propagated by British economist John Maynard Keynes, the architect of the Bretton Woods system. By the 1980s, however, British prime minister Margaret Thatcher and US president Ronald Reagan led the neoliberal revolution against Keynesianism, consciously linking the notion of globalization to the "liberation" of economies around the world.

This new neoliberal economic order received further legitimation with the 1989–91 collapse of communism in the Soviet Union and Eastern Europe. Since then, the three most significant developments related to economic globalization have been the internationalization of trade and finance, the increasing power of transnational corporations, and the enhanced role of international economic institutions like the IMF, the World Bank, and the WTO. Let us briefly examine these important features.

The Internationalization of Trade and Finance

Many people associate economic globalization with the controversial issue of free trade. After all, the total value of world trade exploded from $57 billion in 1947 to an astonishing $12.6 trillion in 2005. In the last few years, the public debate over the alleged benefits and drawbacks of free trade reached a feverish pitch as wealthy northern countries have increased their efforts to establish a single global market through regional and international trade-liberalization agreements such as NAFTA and GATT. Free trade proponents assure the public that the elimination or reduction of existing trade barriers among nations will enhance consumer choice, increase global wealth, secure peaceful international relations, and spread new technologies around the world.

· · · · ·

CONCRETE NEOLIBERAL MEASURES

Concrete neoliberal measures include:

1. Privatization of public enterprises
2. Deregulation of the economy
3. Liberalization of trade and industry
4. Massive tax cuts
5. "Monetarist" measures to keep inflation in check, even at the risk of increasing unemployment
6. Strict control on organized labor
7. The reduction of public expenditures, particularly social spending
8. The downsizing of government
9. The expansion of international markets
10. The removal of controls on global financial flows

· · · · ·

To be sure, there is evidence that some national economies have increased their productivity as a result of free trade. Moreover, there are some benefits that accrue to societies through specialization, competition, and the spread of technology. But it is less clear whether the profits resulting from free trade have been distributed fairly within and among countries. Most studies show that the gap between rich and poor countries is widening at a fast pace. Hence, free trade proponents have encountered severe criticism from labor unions and environmental groups who claim that the elimination of social control mechanisms has resulted in a lowering of global labor standards, severe forms of ecological degradation, and the growing indebtedness of the global South to the North. We will return to the issue of global inequality in Chapters 7 and 8.

The internationalization of trade has gone hand in hand with the liberalization of financial transactions. Its key components include the

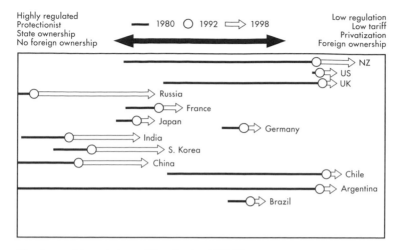

The advance of deregulation and liberalization, 1980–98.

Source: Vincent Cable, *Globalization and Global Governance* (The Royal Institute of International Affairs, 1999), p. 20.

deregulation of interest rates, the removal of credit controls, and the privatization of government-owned banks and financial institutions. Globalization of financial trading allows for increased mobility among different segments of the financial industry, with fewer restrictions and greater investment opportunities. This new financial infrastructure emerged in the 1980s with the gradual deregulation of capital and securities markets in Europe, the Americas, East Asia, Australia, and New Zealand. A decade later, Southeast Asian countries, India, and several African nations followed suit. During the 1990s, new satellite systems and fiber-optic cables provided the nervous system of Internet-based technologies that further accelerated the liberalization of financial transactions. As captured by the snazzy title of Microsoft CEO Bill Gates's best-selling book, many people conducted *business @ the speed of thought*. Millions

The Global South: A Fate Worse Than Debt

Original debt of developing countries in 1980	US$618 billion
Total external debt of developing countries in 2007	US$3.3 trillion
Cost of the war in Iraq to the United States (2003–8)	US$3.3 trillion
Total amount paid by developing countries in debt servicing (1980–2006)	US$7.7 trillion
Amount of debt that the G8 promised to write off	US$100 billion
Amount of debt actually written off so far	US$46 billion
Number of countries eligible for the international Heavily Indebted Poor Countries initiative (HIPC)	42
Proportion of bilateral debt that the G8 countries have promised to cancel for the 42 HIPCs	100%
Proportion of multilateral debt that the World Bank and International Monetary Fund will eventually cancel for the 42 HIPCs	65% (approx.)
Total amount of multilateral debt owed by the 42 HIPCs that is *not* eligible for cancellation	US$93 billion
Amount of money the world's poorest countries spend on debt servicing each year	US$37.5 billion
Profits made by Exxon-Mobil in 2007	US$39.5 billion
Amount of money the United Nations estimates is needed annually to curb the AIDS epidemic in Africa through education, prevention, and care by 2010	US$20–23 billion
Amount of money African nations pay to service their debts each year	US$21 billion
Amount of money wealthy countries spend on defense every year	US$625 billion
Amount of money African countries have paid in debt servicing (1980–2006)	US$675 billion

Amount of money the world's poorest countries spend on debt servicing every 12 days	US$1.25 billion (0.2% of what the rich world spends on defense each year)
Amount of money Kenya owes in external debt (2005)	US$7 billion
Amount of money Kenya allocated to health, water, roads, agriculture, transport, and finance in 2005	US$7 billion
Profits made by Wal-Mart in 2007	US$11.3 billion

Sources: World Bank, *World Development Report 2006: Equity and Development* (World Bank: Washington, DC, 2005); Nakatani and Herera (2007) "The South Has Already Paid Its External Debt to the North," *Monthly Review* 59: 2, http://www. monthlyreview.org/0607pnrh.html (accessed March 18, 2008); Joseph Stiglitz, cited in "Under the Cloud of War" by Daniel Flitton, *Insight* The Age Newspaper, March 15, 2008, p. 4; also on the Web at http://www.theage.com. au/news/in-depth/under-the-cloud-of-war/2008/03/ 14/1205472076737.html; Earth Trends: The Environmental Information Portal, World Resources Institute, http://earthtrends.wri. org (accessed March 15, 2008); Jubilee Debt Campaign UK, June 2006; "HIV/AIDS in Africa 2007–2010: Major Challenges Ahead," Worldpress.org, http://www.worldpress. org/Africa/ 2602.cfm; Fortune magazine top 500 companies, http:// money.cnn.com/magazines/fortune/ fortune500/2007/full_list/index. html (accessed March 18, 2008).

· · · · ·

of individual investors utilized global electronic investment networks not only to place their orders, but also to receive valuable information about relevant economic and political developments. In 2005, Internet publishing, broadcasting, and marketing firms traded approximately $10 trillion in the United States alone.

In 2006, global business-to-business transactions reached US$12.8 trillion. Numerous ventures to connect stock exchanges in different countries have also been attempted in recent years. In early 2007, NASDAQ attempted to take over the London Stock Exchange, offering US$5.3 billion, a move that was rejected by the vast majority of shareholders in the London Stock Exchange. Prior to 2007, however, the New York Stock Exchange (NYSE) established agreements with India's stock exchange and with Tokyo's stock exchange. In April 2007, the NYSE concluded its merger with Euronext NV, creating a business worth US$20 billion. Euronext NV includes stock exchanges in Brussels, Paris, Amsterdam, and Lisbon. In early 2008, the newly merged company announced its plans to take over the American Stock Exchange (AMEX) for US$260 million. It would seem that a global financial supermarket in cyberspace is fast becoming a reality.

· · · · ·

THE SOUTHEAST ASIA CRISIS

In the 1990s, the governments of Thailand, Indonesia, Malaysia, South Korea, and the Philippines gradually abandoned control over the domestic movement of capital in order to attract foreign direct investment. Intent on creating a stable money environment, they raised domestic interest rates and linked their national currencies to the value of the US dollar. The ensuing irrational euphoria of international investors translated into soaring stock and real estate markets all over Southeast Asia. However, by 1997, those investors realized that prices had become inflated much beyond their actual value. They panicked and withdrew a total of $105 billion from these countries, forcing governments in the region to abandon the dollar peg. Unable to halt the ensuing free fall of their currencies, those governments used up their entire foreign exchange reserves. As a result, economic output fell, unemployment increased, and wages plummeted. Foreign banks and creditors reacted by declining new credit applications and refusing to extend existing loans. By late 1997, the entire region found itself in the throes of a financial crisis that threatened to push the global economy into recession.

This disastrous result was only narrowly averted by a combination of international bailout packages and the immediate sale of Southeast Asian commercial assets to foreign corporate investors at rock-bottom prices. Today, ordinary citizens in Southeast Asia are still suffering from the devastating social and political consequences of that economic meltdown. In late 2007 and early 2008, the slowing down of the US economy had serious ramifications for its trading partners in Europe and Asia. It is yet to be seen what the extent of the impact of this will be on the global economy.

· · · · ·

Yet, a large part of the money involved in these global financial exchanges has little to do with supplying capital for such productive investments as putting together machines or organizing raw materials and employees to produce saleable commodities. Most of the financial growth has occurred in the form of high-risk hedge funds and other purely money-dealing currency and securities markets that trade claims to draw profits from future production.

In other words, investors are betting on commodities or currency rates that do not yet exist. For example, in 2007, the equivalent of over US$3 trillion was exchanged daily in global currency markets alone. Dominated by highly sensitive stock markets that drive high-risk innovation, the world's financial systems are characterized by high volatility, rampant competition, and general insecurity. Global speculators often take advantage of weak financial and banking regulations to make astronomical profits in emerging markets of developing countries. However, since these international capital flows can be reversed swiftly, they are capable of creating artificial boom-and-bust cycles that endanger the social welfare of entire regions.

The 1997–98 Southeast Asia crisis represents but one of most serious economic reversals in recent memory brought on by the globalization of financial transactions.

The Power of Transnational Corporations

Transnational corporations are the contemporary versions of the early modern commercial enterprises we discussed in the previous chapter. Powerful firms with subsidiaries in several countries, their numbers skyrocketed from seven thousand in 1970 to about seventy-eight thousand in 2006. Enterprises like General Motors, Wal-Mart, Exxon-Mobil, Mitsubishi, and Siemens belong to the two hundred largest TNCs, which account for over half of the world's industrial output. None of these corporations maintains headquarters outside North America, Europe, Japan, and South Korea. This geographical concentration reflects existing asymmetrical power relations between the North and the South. Yet, clear power differentials can also be found within the global North. In 2005, only one of the top one hundred TNCs worldwide was based in a developing country, Mexico. The rest had their home economies in countries such as the United States, the United Kingdom, Japan, Germany, and France.

Rivaling nation-states in their economic power, these corporations control much of the world's investment capital, technology, and access to international markets. In order to maintain their prominent positions in the global marketplace, TNCs frequently merge with other corporations. Some of these recent mergers include the $160 billion marriage of the world's largest Internet provider, AOL, with entertainment giant Time Warner; the purchase of Chrysler Motors by Daimler-Benz for $43 billion; and the $115 billion merger between Sprint Corporation and

Transnational corporations are the contemporary versions of the British and Dutch East India companies. These powerful firms have subsidiaries in many countries, and none, including global convenience food and beverage firm Pepsi—whose Purchase, New York, headquarters, is pictured here—maintains its headquarters outside the global North.

MCI WorldCom. In 2007, global telecommunications TNCs Nokia and Siemens merged in a deal worth approximately US$38 million. A comparison of GDPs and corporate sales for 2005 reveals that forty-two of the world's one hundred largest economies are corporations; fifty-eight are countries. Hence, it is not surprising that some critics have characterized economic globalization as "corporate globalization" or "globalization from above."

TNCs have consolidated their global operations in an increasingly deregulated global labor market. The availability of cheap labor, resources, and favorable production conditions in the global South has enhanced corporate mobility and profitability. Accounting for over 70 percent of world

Transnational Corporations Versus Countries: A Comparison

CORPORATION	REVENUE ($M)	COUNTRY	GDP ($M)
Wal-Mart Stores	351,139	Sweden	354,115
Exxon-Mobil	347,254	Saudi Arabia	309,778
Royal Dutch Shell	318,845	Austria	304,527
BP	274,316	Denmark	254,401
General Motors	207,349	Greece	213,698
Toyota Motor Corp.	204,746	Ireland	196,388
Chevron	200,567	Thailand	176,602
DaimlerChrysler	190,191	Argentina	183,309
ConocoPhillips	172,451	Portugal	173,085
Total SA	168,357	Venezuela	138,857

Source: Corporations—*Fortune* magazine, July 23, 2007, http://money.cnn.com/magazines/fortune/global500/2007/full_list/index.html; Countries—World Bank, *World Development Report 2007*, pp. 294–95.

· · · · ·

trade, TNCs have boosted their foreign direct investments by approximately 15 percent annually during the 1990s. In 2005, total TNC foreign direct investment amounted to over US$974 billion. Their ability to disperse manufacturing processes into many discrete phases carried out in many different locations around the world reflects the changing nature of global production. Such transnational production networks allow TNCs like Wal-Mart, General Motors, and Volkswagen to produce, distribute, and market their products on a global scale. However, there is also a flip side to the deregulation of the global labor market. Some TNCs have been criticized for maintaining their low prices by condoning poor labor

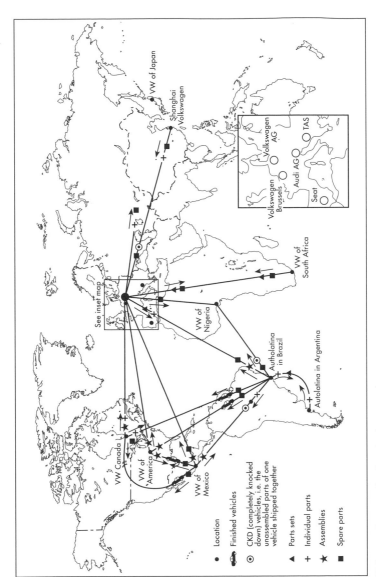

Legend:

- ● Location
- 🚢 Finished vehicles
- ◉ CKD (completely knocked down) vehicles, i.e. the unassembled parts of one vehicle shipped together
- ▲ Parts sets
- + Individual parts
- ★ Assemblies
- ■ Spare parts

Locations shown on map: VW of Japan, Shanghai Volkswagen, VW of South Africa, VW of Nigeria, Autolatina in Brazil, Autolatina in Argentina, VW Canada, VW of America, VW of Mexico, See inset map

Inset map: Volkswagen Brussels, Volkswagen AG, Audi AG, Seat, TAS

Volkswagen's transnational production network.

conditions in the overseas factories that produce the majority of their goods. Some commentators coined the phrase "the race to the bottom" in reference to TNCs' scouring the globe for cheap labor in order to under-sell their competition while keeping their profits high.

· · · · ·

NOKIA'S ROLE IN THE FINNISH ECONOMY

Named after a small town in southwest Finland, Nokia Corporation rose from modest beginnings a little more than a decade ago to become a large TNC that manufactures thirty-seven of every one hundred cell phones sold worldwide. Today, its products connect one billion people in an invisible web around the globe. However, Nokia's gift to Finland—the distinction of being the most inter-connected nation in the world—came at the price of economic dependency. Nokia is the engine of Finland's economy, representing two-thirds of the stock market's value and one-fifth of the nation's total export. It employs twenty-two thousand Finns, not count-ing the estimated twenty thousand domestic employees who work for companies that depend on Nokia contracts. The corporation produces a large part of Finland's tax revenue, and its $25 billion in annual sales almost equals the entire national budget. Yet, when Nokia's growth rate slowed in recent years, company executives let it be known that they were dissatisfied with the country's relatively steep income tax. Today, many Finnish citizens fear that decisions made by relatively few Nokia managers might pressure the govern-ment to lower corporate taxes and abandon the country's generous and egalitarian welfare system. However, it seems that, with its 2007 merger with Siemens (aimed at providing wider telecommu-nications networks and thus increasing business prospects), Nokia is finding creative ways around its slow growth rate without risking the welfare system of Finland.

· · · · ·

No doubt, the growing power of TNCs has profoundly altered the structure and functioning of the international economy. These giant firms and their global strategies have become major determinants of trade flows, the location of industries, and other economic activities around the world. As a consequence, TNCs have become extremely important players that influence the economic, political, and social welfare of many nations. See the box for a final example.

The Enhanced Role of International Economic Institutions

The three international economic institutions most frequently mentioned in the context of economic globalization are the IMF, the World Bank, and the WTO. These three institutions enjoy the privileged position of making and enforcing the rules of a global economy that is sustained by significant power differentials between the global North and South. Since we will discuss the WTO in some detail in Chapter 8, let us focus here on the other two institutions. As pointed out above, the IMF and the World Bank emerged from the Bretton Woods system. During the Cold War, their important function of providing loans for developing countries became connected to the West's political objective of containing communism. Starting in the 1970s, and especially after the fall of the Soviet Union, the economic agenda of the IMF and the World Bank has synchronized neoliberal interests to integrate and deregulate markets around the world.

In return for supplying much-needed loans to developing countries, the IMF and the World Bank demand from their creditor nations the implementation of so-called structural adjustment programs. Unleashed on developing countries in the 1990s, this set of neoliberal policies is often referred to as the "Washington Consensus." It was devised and codified by John Williamson, who was an IMF adviser in the 1970s. The various sections of the program were mainly directed at countries with large foreign debts remaining from the 1970s and 1980s. The official purpose of the document was to reform the internal economic mechanisms of debtor countries in the developing world so that they would be in a better position to repay the debts they had incurred. In practice, however, the terms of the program spelled out a new form of colonialism. The ten points of the Washington Consensus, as defined by Williamson, required governments to implement the following structural adjustments in order to qualify for loans:

1. A guarantee of fiscal discipline, and a curb to budget deficits;
2. A reduction of public expenditure, particularly in the military and public administration;
3. Tax reform, aiming at the creation of a system with a broad base and with effective enforcement;
4. Financial liberalization, with interest rates determined by the market;
5. Competitive exchange rates, to assist export-led growth;
6. Trade liberalization, coupled with the abolition of import licensing and a reduction of tariffs;
7. Promotion of foreign direct investment;
8. Privatization of state enterprises, leading to efficient management and improved performance;
9. Deregulation of the economy;
10. Protection of property rights.

It is no coincidence that this program is called the "Washington Consensus," for, from the outset, the United States has been the dominant power in the IMF and the World Bank. Unfortunately, however, large portions of the "development loans" granted by these institutions either have been pocketed by authoritarian political leaders or have enriched local businesses and the northern corporations they usually serve. Sometimes, exorbitant sums are spent on ill-considered construction projects. Most important, however, structural adjustment programs rarely produce the desired result of "developing" debtor societies, because mandated cuts in public spending translate into fewer social programs, reduced educational opportunities, more environmental pollution, and greater poverty for the vast majority of people. Typically, the largest share of the national budget is spent on servicing outstanding debts. For example, in 2005, developing countries paid US$355,025.5 million in debt servicing, while receiving only US$80,534.1 million in aid. Pressured by anti-corporate globalist forces, the IMF and the World Bank were only recently willing to consider a new policy of blanket debt forgiveness in special cases.

As this chapter has shown, economic perspectives on globalization can hardly be discussed apart from an analysis of political processes and institutions. After all, the intensification of global economic interconnections does not simply fall from the sky; rather, it is set into motion by a series of political decisions. Hence, while acknowledging the importance of economics in our story of globalization, this chapter nonetheless ends with the suggestion that we ought to be skeptical of one-sided accounts that identify expanding economic activity as both the primary aspect of globalization and the engine behind its rapid development. The multidimensional nature of globalization demands that we flesh out in more detail the interaction between its political and economic aspects.

· · · · ·

NEOLIBERAL ECONOMICS AND ARGENTINA

Less than a decade ago, IMF and World Bank officials held up Argentina as a "model developing country." Having accepted substantial structural adjustment programs that led to the privatization of state enterprises, the reduction of tariffs, and the elimination of many social programs, the Argentine government celebrated low unemployment rates, a stable currency pegged to the dollar, and strong foreign investment. For a few short years, neoliberal economics seemed vindicated. However, as the IMF demanded even stronger austerity measures in return for new loans, the Argentine economy went sour. In January 2002, after months of violent street protests in major cities, Argentina formally defaulted on its massive public debt of $141 billion. In order to prevent the complete financial and social collapse of his nation, Eduardo Duhalde, the country's fifth president in only two weeks, further limited people's access to their savings deposits and decoupled the peso from the dollar. Within hours, the currency lost a third of its value, robbing ordinary people of the fruits of their labor. "Argentina is broke, sunk," the president admitted, "and this [neoliberal] model has swept everything away with it." Economic progress since then has been mixed for Argentina. Its GDP has grown substantially at a rate of about 9 percent per year, partially because of debt restructuring and reduced debt burden, excellent international financial conditions, and expansionary monetary and fiscal policies. However, inflation has also continued to grow, reaching double-digit levels in 2006. The government of President Nestor Kirchner responded by implementing price agreements with businesses, as well as export taxes and restraints. Multi-year price freezes on electricity and natural gas rates for residential users stoked consumption and kept private investment away, leading to restrictions on industrial use and blackouts in 2007.

• • • • •

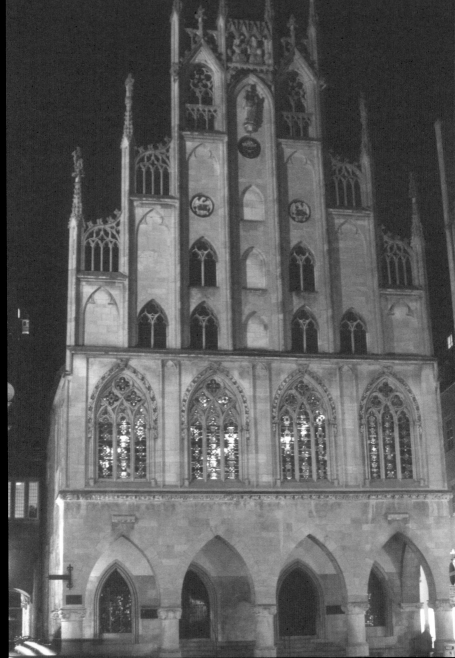

FOUR

The Political Dimension of Globalization

•

POLITICAL GLOBALIZATION refers to the intensification and expansion of political interrelations across the globe. These processes raise an important set of political issues pertaining to the principle of state sovereignty, the growing impact of intergovernmental organizations, and the future prospects for regional and global governance. Obviously, these themes respond to the evolution of political arrangements beyond the framework of the nation-state, thus breaking new conceptual ground. After all, for the last few centuries, humans have organized their political differences along territorial lines that generate a sense of "belonging" to a particular nation-state.

The concept of the nation-state can be traced back to the Peace of Westphalia, which concluded the Thirty Years War and established newly formulated principles of sovereignty and territoriality. Pictured here is the historical town hall in the city of Muenster, Germany, where the Treaty of Muenster, a part of the Peace of Westphalia, was signed.

This artificial division of planetary social space into "domestic" and "foreign" spheres corresponds to people's collective identities based on the creation of a common "us" and an unfamiliar "them." Thus, the modern nation-state system has rested on psychological foundations and cultural assumptions that convey a sense of existential security and historical continuity, while at the same time demanding from its citizens that they put their national loyalties to the ultimate test. Nurtured by demonizing images of the Other, people's belief in the superiority of their own nation has supplied the mental energy required for large-scale warfare—just as the enormous productive capacities of the modern state have provided the material means necessary to fight the "total wars" of the last century.

Contemporary manifestations of globalization have led to the partial permeation of these old territorial borders, in the process also softening hard conceptual boundaries and cultural lines of demarcation. Emphasizing these tendencies, commentators belonging to the camp of hyperglobalizers have suggested that the period since the late 1960s has been marked by a radical "deterritorialization" of politics, rule, and governance. Considering such pronouncements premature at best and erroneous at worst, globalization skeptics not only have affirmed the continued relevance of the nation-state as the political container of modern social life but have also pointed to the emergence of regional blocs as evidence for new forms of territorialization. As each group presents different assessments of the fate of the modern nation-state, they also quarrel over the relative importance of political and economic factors.

Out of these disagreements there have emerged three fundamental questions that probe the extent of political globalization. First, is it really true that the power of the nation-state has been curtailed by massive flows of capital, people, and technology across territorial boundaries?

Second, are the primary causes of these flows to be found in politics or in economics? Third, are we witnessing the emergence of global governance? Before we respond to these questions in more detail, let us briefly consider the main features of the modern nation-state system.

The Modern Nation-State System

The origins of the modern nation-state system can be traced back to seventeenth-century political developments in Europe. In 1648, the Peace of Westphalia concluded a series of religious wars among the main European powers following the Protestant Reformation. Based on the newly formulated principles of sovereignty and territoriality, the ensuing model of self-contained, impersonal states challenged the medieval mosaic of small polities in which political power tended to be local and personal in focus but still subordinated to a larger imperial authority. While the emergence of the Westphalian model did not eclipse the transnational character of vast imperial domains overnight, it nonetheless gradually strengthened a new conception of international law based on the principle that all states had an equal right to self-determination. Whether ruled by absolutist kings in France and Prussia or in a more democratic fashion by the constitutional monarchs and republican leaders of England and the Netherlands, these unified territorial areas constituted the foundation for modernity's secular and national system of political power. According to political scientist David Held, the Westphalian model contained the following essential points:

1. The world consists of, and is divided into, sovereign territorial states which recognize no superior authority.

2. The processes of law making, the settlement of disputes, and law enforcement are largely in the hands of individual states.

3. International law is oriented to the establishment of minimal rules of coexistence; the creation of enduring relationships is an aim, but only to the extent that it allows state objectives to be met.

4. Responsibility for cross-border wrongful acts is a "private matter" concerning only those affected.

5. All states are regarded as equal before the law, but legal rules do not take account of asymmetries of power.

6. Differences among states are often settled by force; the principle of effective power holds sway. Virtually no legal fetters exist to curb the resort to force; international legal standards afford only minimal protection.

7. The collective priority of all states should be to minimize the impediments to state freedom.

The centuries following the Peace of Westphalia saw the further centralization of political power, the expansion of state administration, the development of professional diplomacy, and the successful monopolization of the means of coercion in the hands of the state. Moreover, states also provided the military means required for the expansion of commerce, which, in turn, contributed to the spread of this European form of political rule around the globe. The modern nation-state system found its mature expression at the end of the First World War in US president Woodrow Wilson's famous "Fourteen Points" based on the principle of national self-determination. But his assumption that all forms of national identity should be given their territorial expression in a sovereign "nation-state" proved to be extremely difficult to enforce in practice. Moreover, by enshrining the nation-state as the ethical and legal pinnacle of his proposed interstate system, Wilson unwittingly lent some legitimacy to those radical ethnonationalist forces that pushed the world's main powers into another war of global proportions.

Yet, Wilson's commitment to the nation-state coexisted with his internationalist dream of establishing a global system of collective security under the auspices of a new international organization, the League of Nations. His idea of giving international cooperation an institutional expression was eventually realized with the founding of the United Nations in 1945. While deeply rooted in a political order based on the modern nation-state system, the UN and other fledgling intergovernmental organizations also served as catalysts for the gradual extension of political activities across national boundaries, thus undermining the principle of national sovereignty.

President Woodrow Wilson's Fourteen Points, based on the principle of national self-determination, was the mature expression of the modern-nation state system. The twenty-eighth president of the United States is shown here in a photograph taken between 1914 and 1918.

As globalization tendencies grew stronger during the 1970s, it became clear that the international society of separate states was rapidly turning into a global web of political interdependencies that challenged the sovereignty of nation-states. In 1990, at the outset of the Gulf War, US president George H. W. Bush effectively pronounced dead the Westphalian model

The UN Security Council, charged with maintaining international peace and security, is comprised of fifteen states, five of which—the United States, the United Kingdom, France, Russia, and China—are permanent members. According to Article 25 of the UN Charter, member nations must comply with Security Council Resolutions. This August 6, 1990, photograph shows the Security Council in session.

by announcing the birth of a "new world order" whose leaders no longer respected the idea that cross-border wrongful acts were a matter concerning only those states affected. Did this mean that the modern nation-state system was no longer viable?

The Demise of the Nation-State?

Hyperglobalizers respond to the above question affirmatively. At the same time, most of them consider political globalization a mere secondary phenomenon driven by more fundamental economic and technological forces. They argue that politics has been rendered almost powerless by an unstoppable techno-economic juggernaut that will crush all governmental attempts to reintroduce restrictive policies and regulations. Endowing economics with an inner logic apart from, and superior to, politics, these commentators look forward to a new phase in world history in which the main role of government will be to serve as a superconductor for global capitalism.

Pronouncing the rise of a "borderless world," hyperglobalizers seek to convince the public that globalization inevitably involves the decline of bounded territory as a meaningful concept for understanding political and social change. Consequently, this group of commentators suggests that political power is located in global social formations and expressed through global networks rather than through territorially based states. In fact, they argue that nation-states have already lost their dominant role in the global economy. As territorial divisions are becoming increasingly irrelevant, states are even less capable of determining the direction of social life within their borders. For example, since the workings of genuinely global capital markets dwarf their ability to control exchange rates or protect their currency, nation-states have become vulnerable to the discipline imposed by economic choices made elsewhere, over which states have no practical control. Hyperglobalizers insist that the minimalist political order of the future will be determined by regional economies linked together in an almost seamless global web of production and exchange.

A group of globalization skeptics disagrees, highlighting instead the central role of politics in unleashing the forces of globalization, especially through the successful mobilization of political power. In their view, the rapid expansion of global economic activity can be reduced neither to a natural law of the market nor to the development of computer technology. Rather, it originated with political decisions to lift international restrictions on capital made by neoliberal governments in the 1980s and 1990s. Once those decisions were implemented, global markets and new technologies came into their own. The clear implication of this perspective is that territory still matters. Hence, globalization skeptics insist on the continued relevance of conventional political units, operating in the form of either modern nation-states or global cities.

The arguments of both hyperglobalizers and skeptics remain entangled in a particularly vexing version of the chicken-and-the-egg problem. After all, economic forms of interdependence are set into motion by political decisions, but these decisions are nonetheless made in particular economic contexts. As we have noted in previous chapters, the economic and political aspects of globalization are profoundly interconnected. There is no question that recent economic developments such as trade liberalization and deregulation have significantly constrained the set of political options open to states, particularly in the global South. For example, it has become much easier for capital to escape taxation and other national policy restrictions. Thus, global markets frequently undermine the capacity of governments to set independent national policy objectives and impose their own domestic standards. Hence, we ought to acknowledge the decline of the nation-state as a sovereign entity and the ensuing devolution of state power to regional and local governments as well as to various supranational institutions.

On the other hand, such a concession does not necessarily mean that nation-states have become impotent bystanders to the workings of global forces. Governments can still take measures to make their economies more or less attractive to global investors. In addition, nation-states have retained control over education, infrastructure, and, most important, population movements. Indeed, immigration control, together with population registration and monitoring, has often been cited as the most notable exception to the general trend toward global integration. Although only 2 percent of the world's population live outside their country of origin, immigration control has become a central issue in most advanced nations. Many governments seek to restrict population flows, particularly those originating in the poor countries of the global South. Even in the United States, annual inflows of about six hundred thousand immigrants during the 1990s reached only half the levels recorded during the first two decades of the twentieth century.

Finally, the series of drastic national security measures that were implemented worldwide as a response to the terrorist attacks of 9/11

The 9/11 attacks prompted a worldwide response in the form of heightened security measures. In this photograph taken on February 28, 2003, President George W. Bush shakes hands with Secretary of Homeland Security Tom Ridge at a welcome ceremony for the employees of the newly formed agency. While the department's stated goal is "to secure the country and preserve our freedoms," some civil rights advocates fear that citizens' freedom of movement and assembly may be threatened.

reflect political dynamics that run counter to the hyperglobalizers' predictions of a borderless world. Some civil rights advocates even fear that the enormous resurgence of patriotism around the world might enable states to reimpose restrictions on the freedom of movement and assembly. At the same time, however, the activities of global terrorist networks have revealed the inadequacy of conventional national security structures based on the modern nation-state system, thus forcing national governments to engage in new forms of international cooperation.

Overall, then, we ought to reject premature pronouncements of the impending demise of the nation-state while acknowledging its increasing difficulties in performing some of its traditional functions. Contemporary globalization has weakened some of the conventional boundaries between domestic and foreign policies while fostering the growth of supraterritorial social spaces and institutions that, in turn, unsettle traditional political arrangements. At the outset of the twenty-first century, the world finds itself in a transitional phase between the modern nation-state system and postmodern forms of global governance.

Political Globalization and Global Governance

Political globalization is most visible in the rise of supraterritorial institutions and associations held together by common norms and interests. In this early phase of global governance, these structures resemble an eclectic network of interrelated power centers such as municipal and provincial authorities, regional blocs, international organizations, and national and international private sector associations.

On the municipal and provincial level, there has been a remarkable growth in the number of policy initiatives and transborder links between various substate authorities. For example, Chinese provinces

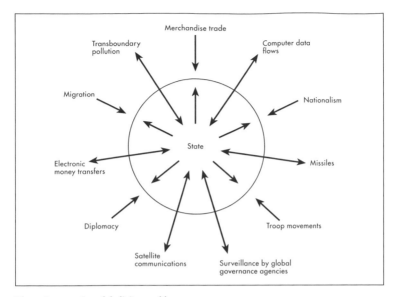

The nation-state in a globalizing world.

Source: Jan Aart Scholte, "The Globalization of World Politics," in John Baylis and Steve Smith (eds.), *The Globalization of World Politics,* 2nd ed. (Oxford University Press, 2001), p. 22.

and US federal states have established permanent missions and points of contact, some of which operate relatively autonomously with little oversight from their respective national governments. Various provinces and federal states in Canada, India, and Brazil are beginning to develop their own trade agendas and financial strategies to obtain loans. An example of international cooperation on the municipal level is the rise of powerful city networks like the World Association of Major Metropolises that develop cooperative ventures to deal with common local issues across national borders. "Global cities" like Tokyo, London, New York, and Singapore tend to be more closely connected to each other than they are to many cities in their home countries.

On the regional level, there has been an extraordinary proliferation of multilateral organizations and agreements. Regional clubs and agencies have sprung up across the world, leading some observers to speculate that they will eventually replace nation-states as the basic unit of governance. Starting out as attempts to integrate regional economies, these regional blocs have, in some cases, already evolved into loose political federations with common institutions of governance. For example, the European Community began in 1950 with French foreign minister Robert Schuman's modest plan to create a supranational institution charged with regulating French and German coal and steel production. Nearly six decades later, twenty-seven member states have formed a close community with political institutions that create common public policies and design binding security arrangements. Following the dissolution of the Soviet Union in 1991, many of the formerly communist countries in Eastern Europe have joined the EU.

On a global level, governments have formed a number of international organizations including the UN, NATO, WTO, and OECD. Full legal membership in these organizations is open to states only, and the decision-making authority lies with representatives from national governments. The proliferation of these transworld bodies has shown that nation-states find it increasingly difficult to manage sprawling networks of social interdependence.

Finally, the emerging structure of global governance is also shaped by "global civil society," a realm populated by thousands of voluntary, nongovernmental associations of worldwide reach. International NGOs like Amnesty International or Greenpeace represent millions of ordinary citizens who are prepared to challenge political and economic decisions made by nation-states and intergovernmental organizations.

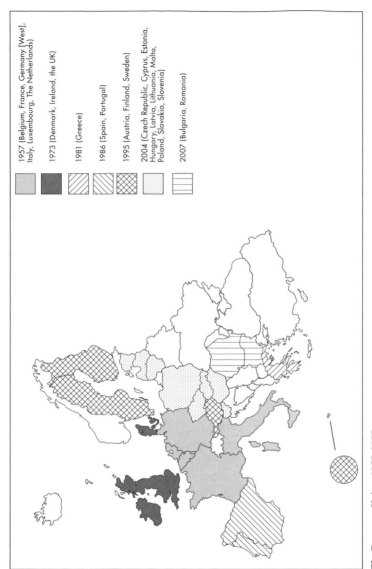

1957 (Belgium, France, Germany [West], Italy, Luxembourg, The Netherlands)

1973 (Denmark, Ireland, the UK)

1981 (Greece)

1986 (Spain, Portugal)

1995 (Austria, Finland, Sweden)

2004 (Czech Republic, Cyprus, Estonia, Hungary, Latvia, Lithuania, Malta, Poland, Slovakia, Slovenia)

2007 (Bulgaria, Romania)

The European Union, 1957–2007.

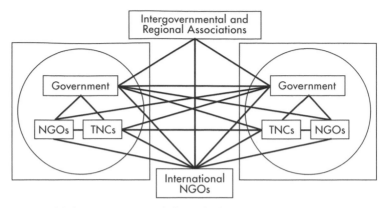

Incipient global governance: a network of interrelated power centers.

Source: Adapted from Peter Willets, "Transnational Actors and International Organizations in Global Politics," in Baylis and Smith (eds.), *The Globalization of World Politics*, 4th ed. (Oxford University Press, 2008), p. 379.

We will examine the justice-globalist activities of some of these organizations in Chapter 7.

Some globalization researchers believe that political globalization might facilitate the emergence of democratic transnational social forces anchored in this thriving sphere of global civil society. Predicting that democratic rights will ultimately become detached from their narrow relationship to discrete territorial units, these optimistic voices anticipate the creation of a democratic global governance structure based on Western cosmopolitan ideals, international legal arrangements, and a web of expanding linkages between various governmental and nongovernmental organizations. If such a promising scenario indeed comes to pass, then the final outcome of political globalization might well be the emergence of a cosmopolitan democracy that would constitute the basis for a plurality of identities flourishing within a structure of mutual toleration and accountability. According to David Held, one of the chief proponents of this view, the cosmopolitan democracy of the future would contain the following political features:

1. A global parliament connected to regions, states, and localities;
2. A new charter of rights and duties locked into different domains of political, social, and economic power;
3. The formal separation of political and economic interests;
4. An interconnected global legal system with mechanisms of enforcement from the local to the global.

A number of less optimistic commentators have challenged the idea that political globalization is moving in the direction of cosmopolitan democracy. Most criticisms boil down to the charge that such a vision indulges in an abstract idealism that fails to engage current political developments on the level of public policy. Skeptics have also expressed the suspicion that the proponents of cosmopolitanism do not consider in sufficient detail the cultural feasibility of global democracy. In other words, the worldwide intensification of cultural, political, and economic interaction makes the possibility of resistance and opposition just as real as the benign vision of mutual accommodation and tolerance of differences. To follow up on this cultural dimension of globalization, let us turn to the next chapter.

A WONDERFUL ANIMATED

OR

MOVING PICTUR

EXHIBITION

ILLUSTRATING THE HIGHEST ATTAINMENT IN THE ART OF PHOTOGRAPH
SHOWING LIFE-SIZE VIEWS OF LIFE AND MOTION

AND A MAGNIFICENT
Stereopticon
Exhibition,
_____ ILLUSTRATING

OUR NEW POSSESSIONS

AND
"FR
CU

THE GREATEST INVENTION OF TH

Animated Pictur

LIFE-LIKE MOTION; LIFE SI

THE WONDERFUL MOVING PICTURE MACHINE
WILL REPRESENT

Scenes and Incidents from the late War with
Railway Trains Going at Full Speed, Man
Scenes, Comic Scenes, Bicycle Parades,

THE OPTIGRAPH MOVING PICTURE MACHINE WILL BE USED.

The Philippines, The Ladrones,
Hawaii and Porto Rico,

ILLUSTRATED THROUGHOUT WITH

52 MAGNIFICENT VIEWS

PROJECTED FROM THE STEREOPTICON.

A Great Combination of Instructive Entertainment and Amusement!

MORE INFORMATION IN TWO HOURS' ENTER-
TAINMENT THAN IN MANY DAYS' READING.

A Most Interesting and Instructive Lecture will be given describing our "New Possessions" BEAUTIFUL HAWAII, THE PHILIPPINES, the Theatre of the Present War; PORTO RICO, the Pearl of the Antilles; THE LADRONES, etc., together with some entirely New Scenes in the Island of Cuba; the natural resources and opportunities for Improvement, Development and Civilization of these FRUITFUL AND BEAUTIFUL COUNTRIES which have lately been acquired by the United States.

THE VIEWS WILL BE ILLUMINATED
By an intense light, magnified by powerful projected onto an immense screen with 100
of surface, making them so large that EVERYONE CAN SEE WHILE COMFORTABLY SEATED IN ANY PART OF THE HALL

There has been a large amount of money spent in collecting authentic and reliable information in securing the

MAGNIFICENT PHOTOGRAPHIC VIE

WE PROMISE YOU A ROYAL ENTERTAINMENT.   DON'T FAIL TO COME AND BRING YOUR FRIENDS.

The Lecture and Entertainment will be given at_____

PRICES OF ADMISSION: ADULTS_____CENTS.   CHILDREN_____

Entertainment begins at 8 P. M._____

FIVE

The Cultural Dimension
of Globalization

•

EVEN AN INTRODUCTION to globalization would be woefully inadequate without an examination of its cultural dimension. Cultural globalization refers to the intensification and expansion of cultural flows across the globe. Obviously, "culture" is a very broad concept; it is frequently used to describe the whole of human experience. In order to avoid the ensuing problem of overgeneralization, it is important to make analytical distinctions between aspects of social life. For example, we associate the adjective "economic" with the production, exchange, and consumption of commodities. If we are discussing the "political," we mean practices related to the generation and distribution of power in societies. If we

Culture **suggests the symbolic construction,** articulation, and dissemination of meaning. Since language, music, and images are major forms of symbolic expression, they take on special significance in the sphere of culture. This moving-picture advertisement is from around 1900.

are talking about the "cultural," we are concerned with the symbolic construction, articulation, and dissemination of meaning. Given that language, music, and images constitute the major forms of symbolic expression, they assume special significance in the sphere of culture.

The exploding network of cultural interconnections and interdependencies in the last decades has led some commentators to suggest that cultural practices lie at the very heart of contemporary globalization. Yet, cultural globalization did not start with the worldwide dissemination of rock 'n' roll, Coca-Cola, or football. As noted in Chapter 2, expansive civilizational exchanges are much older than modernity. Still, the volume and extent of cultural transmissions in the contemporary period have far exceeded those of earlier eras. Facilitated by the Internet and other new technologies, the dominant symbolic systems of meaning of our age—such as individualism, consumerism, and various religious discourses—circulate more freely and widely than ever before. As images and ideas can be more easily and rapidly transmitted from one place to another, they profoundly impact the way people experience their everyday lives. Today, cultural practices frequently escape fixed localities such as town and nation, eventually acquiring new meanings in interaction with dominant global themes.

The thematic landscape traversed by scholars of cultural globalization is vast and the questions they raise are too numerous to be fleshed out in this introduction. Rather than offering a long laundry list of relevant topics, this chapter will focus on three important themes: the tension between sameness and difference in the emerging global culture; the crucial role of transnational media corporations in disseminating popular culture; and the globalization of languages.

Global Culture: Sameness or Difference?

Does globalization make people around the world more alike or more different? This is the question most frequently raised in discussions on the subject of cultural globalization. A group of commentators we might call "pessimistic" hyperglobalizers argue in favor of the former. They suggest that we are not moving toward a cultural rainbow that reflects the diversity of the world's existing cultures. Rather, we are witnessing the rise of an increasingly homogenized popular culture underwritten by a Western "culture industry" based in New York, Hollywood, London, and Milan. As evidence for their interpretation, these commentators point to Amazonian Indians wearing Nike training shoes, denizens of the Southern Sahara purchasing Yankees baseball caps, and Palestinian youths proudly displaying their Chicago

Pessimistic hyperglobalizers argue that we are witnessing the rise of an increasingly homogenized popular culture underwritten by a Western culture industry. In this photograph taken in August 2006, a Tibetan Buddhist lama in Maqu, China, wears Nike socks and carries a bottle of Pepsi.

Bulls sweatshirts in downtown Ramallah. Referring to the diffusion of Anglo-American values and consumer goods as the "Americanization of the world," the proponents of this cultural homogenization thesis argue that Western norms and lifestyles are overwhelming more vulnerable cultures. Although there have been serious attempts by some countries to resist these forces of "cultural imperialism"—for example, a ban on satellite dishes in Iran, and the French imposition of tariffs and quotas on imported film and television—the spread of American popular culture seems to be unstoppable.

But these manifestations of sameness are also evident inside the dominant countries of the global North. American sociologist George Ritzer coined the term "McDonaldization" to describe the wide-ranging sociocultural processes by which the principles of the fast-food restaurant are coming to dominate more and more sectors of American society as well as the rest of the world. On the surface, these principles appear to be rational in their attempts to offer efficient and predictable ways of serving people's needs. However, looking behind the facade of repetitive TV commercials that claim to "love to see you smile," we can identify a number of serious problems. For one, the generally low nutritional value of fast-food meals—and particularly their high fat content—has been implicated in the rise of serious health problems such as heart disease, diabetes, cancer, and juvenile obesity. Moreover, the impersonal, routine operations of "rational" fast-service establishments actually undermine expressions of forms of cultural diversity. In the long run, the McDonaldization of the world amounts to the imposition of uniform standards that eclipse human creativity and dehumanize social relations.

Perhaps the most thoughtful analyst in this group of pessimistic hyperglobalizers is American political theorist Benjamin Barber. In his

The impersonal, routine operations of fast-service establishments, which are spreading throughout American society, can dehumanize social relations. In this recent photograph, bank customers use automatic teller machines.

popular book *Consumed* (2007), he warns his readers against an "ethos of infantilization" that sustains global capitalism, turning adults into children through dumbed-down advertising and consumer goods while also targeting children as consumers. This ethos is premised on the recognition that there is not an endless market for consumerist goods as was once thought. Global inequality contributes to stifling the growth of markets and of capitalism. In order to expand markets and make a profit, global capitalists are developing homogeneous global products targeting the young and wealthy throughout the world, as well as turning children into consumers. Thus, global consumerism becomes increasingly soulless and unethical in its pursuit of profit.

Optimistic hyperglobalizers agree with their pessimistic colleagues that cultural globalization generates more sameness, but they consider this outcome to be a good thing. For example, American social theorist Francis Fukuyama explicitly welcomes the global spread of Anglo-American values and lifestyles, equating the Americanization of the

The American Way of Life

Number of types of packaged bread available at a Safeway in Lake Ridge, Virginia	104
Number of those breads containing no hydrogenated fat or diglycerides	0
Amount of money spent by the fast-food industry on television advertising per year	US$7.2 billion
Amount of money spent promoting the US National Cancer Institute's "Five a Day" program, which encourages the consumption of fruits and vegetables to prevent cancer and other diseases	US $1 million
Number of "coffee drinks" available at Starbucks, whose stores accommodate a stream of over 5 million customers per week, most of whom hurry in and out	61
Number of "coffee drinks" in the 1950s laid-back coffeehouses of Greenwich Village, New York City	2
Number of new models of cars available to suburban residents in 2001	197
Number of convenient alternatives to the car available to most such residents	0
Number of US daily newspapers in 2005	1,452
Number of companies that control the majority of those newspapers	6
Number of leisure hours the average American has per week	35
Number of hours the average American spends watching television per week	30

Sources: Eric Schossler, *Fast Food Nation* (Houghton & Mifflin, 2001), p. 47; http://www.naa.org/info/facts00/11.htm; *Consumer Reports Buying Guide 2001* (Consumers Union, 2001), pp. 147–163; Laurie Garrett, *Betrayal of Trust* (Hyperion, 2000), p. 353; http://www.roper.com/news/content/news169. htm; *The World Almanac and Book of Facts 2008* (World Almanac Books, 2008); http://www.starbucks.com; Project for Excellence in Journalism—State of the News Media 2007, http://www.stateofthenewsmedia.org/2007/chartland.asp?id=169&ct=line&dir=&sort=&col1_box=1&col2_box=1&col3_box= 1&col4_box=1.

world with the expansion of democracy and free markets. But optimistic hyperglobalizers do not just come in the form of American chauvinists who apply the old theme of manifest destiny to the global arena. Some representatives of this camp consider themselves staunch cosmopolitans who celebrate the Internet as the harbinger of a homogenized "technoculture." Others are free-market enthusiasts who embrace the values of global consumer capitalism.

It is one thing to acknowledge the existence of powerful homogenizing tendencies in the world, but it is quite another to assert that the cultural diversity existing on our planet is destined to vanish. In fact, several influential commentators offer a contrary assessment that links globalization to new forms of cultural expression. Sociologist Roland Robertson, for example, contends that global cultural flows often reinvigorate local cultural niches. Hence, rather than being totally obliterated by the Western consumerist forces of sameness, local difference and particularity still play an important role in creating unique cultural constellations. Arguing that cultural globalization always takes place in local contexts, Robertson rejects the cultural homogenization thesis and speaks instead of "glocalization"— a complex interaction of the global and local characterized by cultural borrowing. The resulting expressions of cultural "hybridity" cannot be reduced to clear-cut manifestations of "sameness" or "difference." As we noted in our previous discussion of Osama bin Laden, such processes of hybridization have become most visible in fashion, music, dance, film, food, and language.

Indeed, the respective arguments of hyperglobalizers and skeptics are not necessarily incompatible. The contemporary experience of living and acting across cultural borders means both the loss of traditional

MTV Networks, which has more than twenty channels worldwide, "glocalizes" each channel to bring viewers a popular mixture of international and regional music. In this photograph from 2007, Senegalese American hip-hop artist Akon performs at the launch of MTV Arabia.

meanings and the creation of new symbolic expressions. Reconstructed feelings of belonging coexist in uneasy tension with a sense of placelessness. As we have noted in Chapter 1, cultural globalization has contributed to a remarkable expansion of people's consciousness. It appears that old notions of "national community" are being complemented by the rise of the global imaginary. Indeed, some commentators have argued that modernity is slowly giving way to a new "postmodern" framework characterized by a less stable sense of identity and knowledge.

Given the complexity of global cultural flows, one would actually expect to see uneven and contradictory effects. In certain contexts, these flows might change traditional manifestations of national identity in the direction of a popular culture characterized by sameness; in others they might foster new expressions of cultural particularism; in still others they might encourage forms of cultural "hybridity."

Those commentators who summarily denounce the homogenizing effects of Americanization must not forget that hardly any society in the world today possesses an "authentic," self-contained culture. Those who despair at the flourishing of cultural hybridity ought to listen to exciting Bollywood pop songs, admire the intricacy of several variations of Hawaiian pidgin, or enjoy the culinary delights of Cuban-Chinese cuisine. Finally, those who applaud the spread of consumerist capitalism need to pay attention to its negative consequences, such as the dramatic decline of traditional communal sentiments as well as the commodification of society and nature.

The Role of the Media

To a large extent, the global cultural flows of our time are generated and directed by global media empires that rely on powerful communication technologies to spread their message. Saturating global cultural reality with formulaic TV shows and mindless advertisements, these corporations increasingly shape people's identities and the structure of desires around the world. The rise of the global imaginary is inextricably connected to the rise of the global media. During the last two decades, a small group of very large TNCs have come to dominate the global market for entertainment, news, television, and film. In 2006, only eight media conglomerates—Yahoo, Google, AOL-Time Warner, Microsoft, Viacom, General Electric, Disney, and News Corporation—accounted for more than two-thirds of the $250–$275 billion in annual worldwide revenues generated by the communications industry. In the first half of that year, the volume of merger deals in global media, Internet, and telecommunications totaled $300 billion, three times the figure for the first six months of 1999.

As recently as fifteen years ago, not one of the giant corporations that dominate what Benjamin Barber has appropriately called the "infotainment telesector" existed in its present form as a media company. In 2001, nearly all of these corporations ranked among the largest three hundred nonfinancial firms in the world. Today, most media analysts concede that the emergence of a global commercial-media market amounts to the creation of a global oligopoly similar to that of the oil and automotive industries in the early part of the twentieth century. The crucial cultural innovators of earlier decades—small, independent record labels, radio stations, movie theaters, newspapers, and book publishers—have become virtually extinct as they found themselves incapable of competing with the media giants.

The negative consequences of this shotgun marriage of finance and culture are obvious. TV programs turn into global "gossip markets," presenting viewers and readers of all ages with the vacuous details of the private lives of American celebrities like Britney Spears, Jennifer Lopez,

Justin Timberlake, and Matt Damon. Evidence suggests that people all over the world—but especially those from wealthy countries of the Northern Hemisphere—are watching more television than ever before. For example, the daily average viewing time per TV home in the United States has increased from five hours and fifty-six minutes in 1970 to seven hours and twenty-six minutes in 1999. That same year, TV household penetration in the United States stood at a record 98.3 percent, with 73.9 percent of TV households owning two or more sets. Advertisement clutter on US television reached unprecedented levels in 2000, peaking at over fifteen minutes of commercials per prime-time TV hour, not including the frequent cutaways for local ads. The TV advertisement volume in the United States has increased from $3.60 billion in 1970 to $50.44 billion in 1999. Recent studies show that American children at age twelve watch

Over the past few decades, a small group of very large TNCs has come to dominate the global market for entertainment, news, television, and film. In this photograph taken around 1927, D. E. Replogle gives the first public demonstration of talking moving pictures being transmitted over radio without the use of land wires from the studio of the Jenkins Television Corporation in Jersey City, New Jersey. By the early twenty-first century, twelve-year-old American children were watching an average of twenty thousand television commercials a year.

an average of twenty thousand TV commercials a year, and two-year-old toddlers have already developed brand loyalties.

The values disseminated by transnational media enterprises not only secure the undisputed cultural hegemony of popular culture, but also lead to the depoliticization of social reality and the weakening of civic bonds. One of the most glaring developments of the last two decades has been the transformation of news broadcasts and educational programs into shallow entertainment shows. Given that news is less than half as profitable as entertainment, media firms are increasingly tempted to pursue higher profits by ignoring journalism's much vaunted separation of newsroom practices and business decisions. Partnerships and alliances between news and entertainment companies are fast becoming the norm, making it more common for publishing executives to press journalists to cooperate with their newspapers' business operations. A sustained attack on the professional autonomy of journalism is, therefore, also part of cultural globalization.

The Globalization of Languages

One direct method of measuring and evaluating cultural changes brought about by globalization is to study the shifting global patterns of language use. The globalization of languages can be viewed as a process by which some languages are increasingly used in international communication while others lose their prominence and even disappear for lack of speakers. Researchers at the Globalization Research Center at the University of Hawaii have identified five key variables that influence the globalization of languages:

1. *Number of languages*: The declining number of languages in different parts of the world points to the strengthening of homogenizing cultural forces.

2. *Movements of people*: People carry their languages with them when they migrate and travel. Migration patterns affect the spread of languages.

3. *Foreign-language learning and tourism*: Foreign-language learning and tourism facilitate the spread of languages beyond national or cultural boundaries.

4. *Internet languages*: The Internet has become a global medium for instant communication and quick access to information. Language use on the Internet is a key factor in the analysis of the dominance and variety of languages in international communication.

5. *International scientific publications*: International scientific publications contain the languages of global intellectual discourse, thus critically impacting intellectual communities involved in the production, reproduction, and circulation of knowledge around the world.

Given these highly complex interactions, research in this area frequently yields contradictory conclusions. The figure above represents only one possible conceptualization of the meaning and effects of language globalization. Unable to reach a general agreement, experts in the field have developed several different hypotheses. One model posits a clear correlation between the growing global significance of a few languages—particularly English, Chinese, and Spanish—and the declining number of other languages around the world. Another model suggests that the globalization of language does not necessarily mean that our descendants are destined to utilize only a few tongues. Still another thesis emphasizes the power of the Anglo-American culture industry to make English *the* global lingua franca of the twenty-first century.

To be sure, the rising significance of the English language has a long history, reaching back to the birth of British colonialism in the late

The Declining Number of Languages Around the World, 1500–2000

CONTINENTS	EARLY 16TH CENTURY		EARLY 17TH CENTURY		EARLY 18TH CENTURY		EARLY 19TH CENTURY		EARLY 20TH CENTURY		LATE 20TH CENTURY		EARLY 21ST CENTURY	
	Number	%	Number	%	Number	%	Number	%	Number	%	Number	%	Number	%
Americas	2,175	15	2,025	15	1,800	15	1,500	15	1,125	15	1,005	15	336	12
Africa	4,350	30	4,050	30	3,600	30	3,000	30	2,250	30	2,011	30	1,355	45
Europe	435	3	405	3	360	3	300	3	225	3	201	3	140	5
Asia	4,785	33	4,455	33	3,960	33	3,300	33	2,475	33	2,212	33	1,044	38
Pacific	2,755	19	2,565	19	2,280	19	1,900	19	1,425	19	1,274	19	92	3
World	14,500	100	13,500	100	12,000	100	10,000	100	7,500	100	6,703	100	2,967	100

Source: Globalization Research Center at the University of Hawaii-Manoa, http://www.globalhawaii.org.

sixteenth century. At that time, only approximately 7 million people used English as their mother tongue. By the 1990s, this number had swollen to over 350 million native speakers, with 400 million more using English as a second language. Today, more than 80 percent of the content posted on the Internet is in English. Almost half of the world's growing population of foreign students are enrolled at institutions in Anglo-American countries.

At the same time, however, the number of spoken languages in the world has dropped from about 14,500 in 1500 to less than 7,000 in 2007. Given the current rate of decline, some linguists predict that 50–90 percent of the currently existing languages will have disappeared by the end of the twenty-first century. But the world's languages are not the only entities threatened with extinction. The spread of consumerist values and materialist lifestyles has endangered the ecological health of our planet as well.

Let us now explore the ecological dimension of globalization, which has received much attention in recent years.

In the process of analyzing the globalization of languages, one school of thought predicts that the power of Anglo-American culture will make English the global lingua franca of the twenty-first century. In this photograph from Shenyang, China, young Chinese gather to hold English Corner, a regular meeting of Chinese people who want to practice their spoken English.

SIX

The Ecological Dimension
of Globalization

●

ALTHOUGH WE HAVE EXAMINED the economic, political, and cultural aspects of globalization separately, it is important to emphasize that each of these dimensions impacts on and has consequences for the other domains. Nowhere is this more clearly demonstrated than in the ecological dimensions of globalization. In recent years, global environmental issues have received enormous attention from research institutes, the media, politicians, and economists. Indeed, the ecological impacts of globalization are increasingly recognized as the most

The global population has exploded a thousandfold to more than six billion since the advent of farming economies, dramatically increasing demands for food, timber, and fiber and putting severe pressure on the planet's ecosystems. This photograph, taken in 2007 in Euberta, New South Wales, Australia, shows the center-pivot method of irrigation, used in dry areas to promote crop production.

significant and potentially life threatening for the world as we have inherited it from our ancestors.

In addition to economic and political factors, cultural values and background greatly influence how people view their natural environment. For example, cultures steeped in Taoist, Buddhist, and various animist religions tend to emphasize the interdependence of all living beings—a perspective that calls for a delicate balance between human wants and ecological needs. Judeo-Christian humanism, on the other hand, contains deeply dualistic values that put human beings at the center of the universe. In modernity, nature has come to be considered as a "resource" to be used instrumentally to fulfill human desires. The most extreme manifestation of this "anthropo-centric" paradigm is reflected in the dominant values and beliefs of consumerism. As pointed out previously, the US-dominated culture industry seeks to convince its global audience that the meaning and chief value of life can be found in the limitless accumulation of material possessions.

At the dawn of the twenty-first century, however, it has become virtually impossible to ignore the fact that people everywhere on this planet are inextricably linked to each other through the air they breathe, the climate they depend upon, the food they eat, and the water they drink. In spite of this obvious lesson of interdependence, our planet's ecosystems are subjected to continuous human assault in order to maintain wasteful lifestyles. Granted, some of the major ecological challenges the world faces today are problems that afflicted civilizations even in ancient times. But until the coming of the Industrial Revolution, environmental degradation was relatively localized and occurred rather slowly over many centuries.

In the last few decades, however, the scale, speed, and depth of Earth's environmental decline have been unprecedented. Let us briefly consider some of the most dangerous manifestations of the globalization of environmental degradation.

Two of the major concerns relate to uncontrolled population growth and lavish consumption patterns, particularly in the global North. Since farming economies first came into existence about 480 generations ago, the global population has exploded a thousandfold to more than six billion. Half of this increase has occurred in the last thirty years. With the possible exception of some rodent species, humans are now the most numerous mammals on earth. Vastly increased demands for food, timber, and fiber have put severe pressure on the planet's ecosystems.

Large areas of the Earth's surface, especially in arid and semi-arid regions, have been used for agricultural production for millennia, yielding crops for ever-increasing numbers of people. Concerns about the relationship between population growth and environmental degradation are frequently focused rather narrowly on aggregate population levels. Yet, the global impact of humans on the environment is as much a function of per capita consumption as it is of overall population size. For example, the United States comprises only 6 percent of the world's population, but it consumes 30–40 percent of our planet's natural resources. Global overconsumption and uncontrolled population growth present a serious problem to the environment. Unless we are willing to change the underlying cultural and religious value structure that has combined with the social and economic dynamics of unrestrained capitalist accumulation, the health of Mother Earth is likely to deteriorate even further.

Some of the effects of overconsumption and population growth are painfully obvious in the current food crisis plaguing vast regions of

Annual Consumption Patterns (Per Capita) in Selected Countries in 2001

COUNTRY	MEAT (KG)	PAPER (KG)	FOSSIL FUELS (KG OF OIL EQUIVALENT)	PASSENGER CARS (PER 1,000 PEOPLE)	TOTAL VALUE OF PRIVATE CONSUMPTION (IN US DOLLARS)
USA	122	293	6,902	489	21,680
Japan	42	239	3,277	373	15,554
Poland	73	54	2,585	209	5,087
China	47	30	700	3.2	1,410
Zambia	12	1.6	77	17	625

Source: US Public Broadcasting Service, http://www.pbs.org/earthonedge/science/trends.html.

• • • • •

our planet. Food riots in Haiti, Indonesia, the Philippines, China, and Cameroon in 2008 highlight increasing limitations on access to food in part as a result of environmental problems such as drought. Other factors include rising oil prices (which affect the cost of transportation of food), diversion of food staples such as corn into production of biofuels in efforts to reduce reliance on oil, and unequal access to resources across developed and developing countries. On the one hand, the worsening food crisis highlights the interconnections between political, economic, and ecological problems. Indeed, globalization processes such as the expansion of trade and transport drive overconsumption and environmental degradation. But, on the other hand, the food crisis also shows how global responses to environmental problems may also lead to new problems such as the aforementioned biofuel issue or the considerable risks associated with nuclear alternatives to carbon-based energy sources.

Ironically, such attempts to reduce our species' "carbon footprint" contain different threats to the environment.

Another significant ecological problem associated with population increases and the globalization of environmental degradation is the worldwide reduction of biodiversity. Seven out of ten biologists today believe that the world is now in the midst of the fastest mass extinction of living species in the 4.5-billion-year history of the planet. According to recent OECD reports, two-thirds of the world's farmlands have been rated as "somewhat degraded" and one-third have been marked as "strongly degraded." Half the world's wetlands have already been destroyed, and the biodiversity of freshwater ecosystems is under serious threat. Three-quarters of worldwide genetic diversity in agricultural crop and animal breeds has been lost since 1900. Some experts fear that up to 50 percent of all plant and animal species—most of them in the global South—will disappear by the end of this century.

Almost three-quarters of biologists believe that the world is in the midst of the fastest mass extinction of living species in the earth's history. The Fijian crested iguana, which turns from the bright green pictured here in a recent photograph to jet-black when it is alarmed, is one of the many of the world's endangered species.

Transboundary pollution represents another grave danger to our collective survival. The release of vast amounts of synthetic chemicals into the air and water has created conditions for human and animal life that are outside previous limits of biological experience. For example, chlorofluorocarbons have been used in the second half of the twentieth century as nonflammable refrigerants, industrial solvents, foaming agents, and aerosol propellants. In the mid-1970s, researchers noted that the unregulated release of CFCs into the air seemed to be depleting Earth's protective ozone layer. A decade later, the discovery of large "ozone holes" over Tasmania, New Zealand, and large parts of the Antarctic finally resulted in a coordinated international effort to phase out production of CFCs and other ozone-depleting substances. Other forms of transboundary pollution include industrial emissions of sulfur and nitrogen oxides. Returning to the ground in the form of "acid rain," these chemicals damage forests, soils, and freshwater ecosystems. Current acid deposits in Northern Europe and parts of North America are at least twice as high as the critical level suggested by environmental agencies.

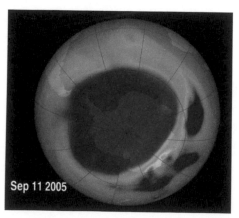

Sep 11 2005

In the mid-1970s, scientists discovered that the unregulated release of CFCs into the atmosphere was depleting the ozone layer, which protects the earth from harmful ultraviolet rays. This NASA graphic shows the dramatic thinning (the "hole") in the ozone layer over Antarctica.

Finally, in the last few years, the issue of human-induced climate change has been a major focus of domestic and intergovernmental policy as well as grassroots activism. Brought to enhanced public attention by former US vice president Al Gore through his award-winning documentary, *An Inconvenient Truth*, as well as the production of numerous scientific reports outlining the dire consequences of unchecked global warming, climate change has emerged as one of the top three global problems facing humanity today. The consequences of worldwide climate change, especially global warming, could be catastrophic. Many scientists are calling for immediate action by governments to curb greenhouse gas emissions.

Indeed, global warming represents a grim example of the decisive shift in both the intensity and extent of contemporary environmental problems. The rapid buildup of gas emissions, including carbon dioxide, methane, nitrous and sulfur oxides, and chlorofluorocarbons in our planet's atmosphere has greatly enhanced Earth's capacity to trap heat. The resulting enhanced "greenhouse effect" is responsible for raising average temperatures worldwide.

The precise social effects of global climate change are difficult to calculate. In 2006, Sir Nicholas Stern, former chief economist for the World Bank, released one of the most comprehensive and alarming reports on both the expected extent and economic impacts of climate change. The "Stern Report," commissioned by the UK government, asserts that average global temperatures have already risen by 0.9 degrees Fahrenheit (0.5 degrees Celsius) based on pre-industrialization temperatures. Based on current trends, average global temperatures will rise by an additional 3 to 6 degrees Fahrenheit (2 to 3 degrees Celsius) over the next fifty to seventy-five years. In the next century, they might rise another 6 degrees

Fahrenheit (3 degrees Celsius). In some parts of Africa, the average temperature has already risen by more than 1.8 degrees Fahrenheit (1 degree Celsius) in the last twenty years.

Further increases in global temperatures could lead to partial meltdowns of the polar ice caps, causing global sea levels to rise by up to thirty-five inches (ninety centimeters) by 2100. In an interview published in Britain's *Sun* newspaper in April 2008, Al Gore warned that the entire North Polar ice cap is melting more rapidly than expected and could be gone in large areas in as little as ten years. Since the North Pole ice is not on land, but floating in the sea, it will not change sea levels. Still, it will be of great concern for global transport and access to oil, gas, and mineral reserves, thus breeding geopolitical conflict. The melting of the Greenland ice sheet, however, is emerging as a much greater concern for global sea levels. The implications of this process for many coastal regions around the world would be catastrophic. The small Pacific island nations of Tuvalu and Kiribati would be completely wiped out. Large coastal

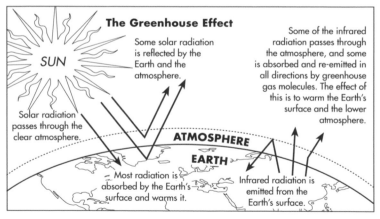

The greenhouse effect.

cities such as Tokyo, New York, London, and Sydney would lose significant chunks of their urban landscapes.

The central feature of all these potentially disastrous environmental problems is that they are "global issues."

Transboundary pollution, global warming, climate change, and species extinction are challenges that cannot be contained within national or even regional borders. They do not have isolated causes and effects. They are global problems, caused by aggregate collective human actions, and thus require a coordinated global response. To be sure, ecological problems aggravated by globalization also have significant economic ramifications. Although these effects will be more significant for less developed countries than for rich countries, they will nonetheless affect all people and all nations.

Poor countries do not have the necessary infrastructure or income to adapt to the unavoidable climate changes that will occur because of

Major manifestations and consequences of global environmental degradation.

The Top 20 Carbon Dioxide Emitters

COUNTRY	TOTAL EMISSIONS (1,000 TONS OF C)	PER CAPITA EMISSIONS (TONS/CAPITA)	PER CAPITA EMISSIONS (RANK)
1. United States	1,650,020	5.61	9
2. China (mainland)	1,366,554	1.05	92
3. Russian Federation	415,951	2.89	28
4. India	366,301	0.34	129
5. Japan	343,117	2.69	33
6. Germany	220,596	2.67	36
7. Canada	174,401	5.46	10
8. United Kingdom	160,179	2.67	37
9. Republic of Korea	127,007	2.64	39
10. Italy (including San Marino)	122,726	2.12	50
11. Mexico	119,473	1.14	84
12. South Africa	119,203	2.68	34
13. Iran	118,259	1.76	63
14. Indonesia	103,170	0.47	121
15. France (including Monaco)	101,927	1.64	66
16. Brazil	90,499	0.50	118
17. Spain	90,145	2.08	52
18. Ukraine	90,020	1.90	56
19. Australia	89,125	4.41	13
20. Saudi Arabia	84,116	3.71	18

Source: Marland, Boden, and Andres, "Global, Regional and National CO_2 Emissions," in *Trends: A Compendium of Data on Global Change* (Carbon Dioxide Information Analysis Center, Oak Ridge National Laboratory, US Department of Energy, Oak Ridge, Tennessee, 2004); available online at http://cdiac.esd.ornl.gov/trends/emis/tre_coun.htm.

Note: Quantities are in metric tons; 1 metric ton = 1.1 short tons.

• • • • •

carbon emissions already in the earth's atmosphere. As we noted above, developing regions are already warmer on average than many developing countries that are located in the semi-arid tropics, where rainfall variability is higher. To make matters worse, less developed countries are also heavily dependent on agriculture for the majority of their income. Since agriculture is the most climate sensitive of all economic sectors, developing nations will be more adversely affected by climate change than developed countries. Further consequences of this vicious circle include increased illnesses, escalating death rates, and crumbling infrastructure. The cost of living will continue to rise, leaving poor households and communities unable to save for future emergencies. Recent scientific reviews like the Stern Report consider the implications of climate change for development and aid. No doubt, the global South will require significant assistance from the developed world if it is to adapt and survive climate change. Indeed, these issues are not merely environmental or scientific matters. They are economic, political, cultural, but above all ethical issues that have been expanded and intensified by globalization processes.

There has been much debate in public and academic circles about the severity of climate change and the best ways for the global community to respond to it. As can be gleaned from the list of major global environmental treaties provided below, international discussion on the issue of global warming and environmental degradation has been occurring for over thirty years. Yet, while much has been written and spoken about this issue, few coordinated measures have been implemented. Most international environmental treaties lack effective enforcement mechanisms.

For the most part, political will in favor of immediate change has been weak and limited. However, the most significant obstacles to the creation and implementation of an effective global environmental agreement has come from the unwillingness of China and the United States—the world's two largest polluters—to ratify key agreements. Both nations see measures to reduce carbon emissions and thereby slow global warming as threats to their economic growth. Yet inaction on climate change today will have more dire consequences for economic growth tomorrow.

Still, there are some grounds for guarded optimism. For example, significant agreement exists that certain limitations on carbon emissions must be placed on all nations. Yet, poor countries argue that they should not be bound by the same limits as developed countries. They make this argument for two reasons. First, they need to build up their industries and infrastructures in order to pull themselves out of poverty. Placing significant carbon emissions restrictions on their industries would seriously impede their economic development. Second, they argue that poor countries have not been responsible for the production of most of the greenhouse gases that have caused the current problem. Identifying developed countries as the primary producers of greenhouse gases, they suggest that the major burden for limiting the production of greenhouse gases should fall on the developed world—at least until developing countries have pulled their populations out of extreme poverty.

The United States has expressed strong opposition to these arguments by insisting that all countries should be subjected to the same limitations on carbon emissions. At the Thirteenth Conference of the Parties (COP 13) to the United Nations Framework Convention on Climate Change (UNFCCC) in Bali 2007, the US delegation repeatedly blocked negotiations by demanding that developing countries take more responsibility for their contribution to global warming. At the same time,

Major Global Environmental Treaties, 1971–2007

NAME OF TREATY	COVERAGE/PROTECTION	DATE
Ramsar Convention	Iran Wetlands	1971
UNESCO-World Heritage, Paris	Cultural and natural heritage	1972
UNEP Conference, Stockholm	General environment	1972
CITES, Washington, DC	Endangered species	1973
Marine Pollution Treaty, London	Marine pollution from ships	1978
UN Convention on Law of the Sea	Marine species, pollution	1982
Vienna Protocol	Ozone layer	1985
Montreal Protocol	Ozone layer	1987
Basel Convention	Hazardous wastes	1989
UN "Rio Summit" on Environmental Climate Change	Biodiversity	1992
Jakarta Mandate	Marine and coastal diversity	1995
Kyoto Protocol	Global warming	1997
Rotterdam Convention	Industrial pollution	1998
Johannesburg World Summit	Ecological sustainability, pollution	2002
Bali Action Plan	Global warming	2007

· · · · ·

however, America has been reluctant to enter into any agreement that might slow its own economic growth. The Bush administration has walked away from key international treaties such as the Kyoto Protocol while remaining significantly behind other developed countries in its commitments on capping and reducing carbon emissions. Although the US president has made some alternative efforts to address climate change by implementing some suggestions emerging from the Major Economies Meeting on Energy and Climate Change, his efforts are seen by most as too little, too late. This is exemplified by a statement made by George W. Bush in 2008 in which he sets the year 2025 as the year in which US carbon emissions would peak, with no mention of when they would actually begin to fall. Most leading scientists believe that a further decade of inaction would make it impossible to avoid the disastrous impacts of climate change.

Without the full participation and backing of one of the world's major polluters and the world's most powerful political and military power, many commentators hold little hope for reaching consensus and implementing global action on climate change. As a result of its posture, the United States is being increasingly isolated at international climate change meetings. At the COP 13, for example, the American delegation was mocked, booed, and jeered by many delegates from the developing world. US demands even failed to receive support from its traditional allies, such as Japan, Canada, Australia, and New Zealand. Eventually, the US delegation was forced to accept consensus. Perhaps the impending end of the Bush era will allow for a new approach to climate change in America. Fortunately, public opinion on climate change in the US is changing rapidly. The majority of US citizens now rank climate change and global warming as one of their major concerns for the immediate future. Moreover, much of the effort to address global climate change occurs at the subnational level. For example, major American cities have passed eco-friendlier laws, and similar measures enjoy large, bipartisan support from state legislators in California and other large states.

Other developed countries have already taken a lead in implementing strategies for reducing carbon emissions. The EU, for example, has implemented a successful carbon-trading scheme used as a model by other nations. Indeed, the 2006 Stern Report proposed expanding the EU scheme to include as many countries as possible. Other policy proposals of this UK-commissioned report include support for the development of a range of low-carbon and high-efficiency technologies, removal of barriers to behavioral change, adaptation policy, and curbing deforestation. Taking these pointers seriously, the UK government has already committed to a 60 percent reduction in carbon emissions by 2050.

The next major international agreement on climate change is due to be negotiated in 2009 at the Copenhagen Conference of the Parties under the United Nations Climate Change Convention. The likely agreement drawn up at this meeting would come into effect in 2012 with the lapse of the Kyoto Protocol. Scientists, economists, and politicians from around the world have emphasized that the global community must take drastic and immediate action if the worst effects of climate change are to be avoided. For better or worse, human-made environmental degradation has emerged as both a powerful cause and effect of globalization. Hopefully, the 2009 Copenhagen Meeting will enhance global cooperation on this crucial global issue. But it remains to be seen whether the growing recognition of the ecological limits of our planet will translate into a much-needed revision of ideologies rooted in the desire for the unlimited accumulation of material things.

RESIST CORPORATE TYRANNY

WTO

JUST SAY NO!

THE PEOPLE HAVE SPOKEN!

This sign made possible by NAKED CLOTHING

SEVEN

Ideologies of Globalization: Market Globalism, Justice Globalism, Jihadist Globalism

●

IDEOLOGIES ARE POWERFUL SYSTEMS of widely shared ideas and patterned beliefs that are accepted as truth by significant groups in society. They offer people a more or less coherent picture of the world not only as it is, but also as it ought to be. In doing so, ideologies help organize the tremendous complexity of human experience into fairly simple claims that serve as guide and compass for social and political action. These claims are employed to legitimize certain political interests and to defend

The ideological dimension of globalization covers a range of norms, claims, beliefs, and narratives about the phenomenon itself. This photograph taken at the November 30, 1999, Seattle protests against the WTO shows activists blocking one of the main roads in the city to slow down the opening of the summit.

or challenge dominant power structures. Seeking to imbue society with their preferred norms and values, the codifiers of ideologies—usually social elites—provide the public with a circumscribed agenda of things to discuss, claims to make, and questions to ask. These power elites speak to their audience in narratives that persuade, praise, condemn, distinguish "truths" from "falsehoods," and separate the "good" from the "bad." Thus, ideology connects theory and practice by orienting and organizing human action in accordance with generalized claims and codes of conduct.

Like all social processes, globalization operates on an ideological dimension filled with a range of norms, claims, beliefs, and narratives about the phenomenon itself. Indeed, the heated public debate over whether globalization represents a "good" or a "bad" thing occurs in the arena of ideology. But before we explore the ideological dimension of globalization in more detail, we should recall our important analytical distinction between *globalization*—a set of social processes of intensifying global interdependence—and *globalisms*—ideologies that endow the concept of globalization with particular values and meanings.

Today, three types of globalism compete for adherents around the globe. *Market globalism* seeks to endow "globalization" with free-market norms and neoliberal meanings. Contesting market globalism from the political Left, *justice globalism* constructs an alternative vision of globalization based on egalitarian ideals of global solidarity and distributive justice. From the political Right, *jihadist globalism* struggles against both market globalism and justice globalism as it seeks to mobilize the global *umma* (Muslim community of believers) in defense of allegedly Islamic values and beliefs that are thought to be under severe attack by the forces of secularism and consumerism. In spite of their considerable differences, however, these three globalisms share nonetheless an important function: they articulate and translate the rising global imaginary—notions of community increasingly tied to the global—into concrete political programs and agendas. Hence, it would be inaccurate to accuse the two ideological challengers of market globalism of being "antiglobalization." Rather, their position could be described as "alter-globalization"—an alternative vision that resists dominant neoliberal projections of an integrated world based on free-market principles.

To be sure, there are powerful voices of "antiglobalization"— inveterate nationalists and economic protectionists—such as Pat Buchanan in the United States, Jean-Marie Le Pen in France, or Pauline Hanson in Australia. Buchanan, for example, supports in his best-selling books and fiery political speeches "economic nationalism"— the view that the economy should be designed in ways that serve narrow national interests. He frequently expresses the conviction that

Patrick Buchanan is a prominent representative of the US economic protectionist position. In this photograph taken on February, 29, 1996, Buchanan speaks at a Christian Coalition Rally.

there exists at the core of contemporary American society an irrepressible conflict between the claims of American nationalism and the commands of the global economy.

In Buchanan's opinion, most mainstream American politicians are beholden to transnational corporate interests that are undermining the sovereignty of the nation by supporting a global governance structure headed by the WTO and other international institutions. He also accuses "globalist advocates of multiculturalism" of opening the doors to millions of immigrants who are allegedly responsible for the economic and moral decline of the United States.

Fearing the loss of national self-determination and the destruction of their national cultures, antiglobalization voices like Buchanan pledge to protect their nation from those "foreign elements" they consider responsible for unleashing the forces of globalization. Clinging to the weakening national imaginary, they regard autonomous nation-states as the only legitimate form of community. Hence, antiglobalists can be viewed as "reactionaries" in the sense of reacting against all three globalist ideologies without providing their national audiences with constructive articulations of the rising global imaginary.

Market Globalism

Market globalism is without question the dominant ideology of our time. Over the last three decades, it has been codified and disseminated worldwide by global power elites that include corporate managers, executives of large transnational corporations, corporate lobbyists, influential journalists and public-relations specialists, intellectuals writing for a large public audience, celebrities and top entertainers, state bureaucrats, and politicians.

Microsoft CEO Bill Gates, shown here in a photograph taken in 2000 at a computer trade show, is one of the world's most powerful advocates of globalism.

Serving as the chief advocates of market globalism, these individuals saturate the public discourse with idealized images of a consumerist, free-market world. Selling their preferred version of a single global marketplace to the public, they portray globalization in a positive light as an indispensable tool for the realization of such a global order. Such favorable visions of globalization pervade public opinion and political choices in many parts of the world. Indeed, neoliberal decision makers emerged as expert designers of an attractive ideological container for their market-friendly political agenda. Given that the exchange of commodities constitutes the core activity of all societies, the market-oriented discourse of globalization itself has turned into an extremely important commodity destined for public consumption. *Business Week*, the *Economist*, *Forbes*, the *Wall Street Journal*, and the *Financial Times* are among the most powerful of dozens of magazines, journals, newspapers, and electronic media published globally that feed their readers a steady diet of market-globalist claims.

Thus, market globalism has become what some social theorists call a "strong discourse"—one that is notoriously difficult to resist and repel because it has on its side powerful social forces that have already preselected what counts as "real" and, therefore, shape the world accordingly. The constant repetition and public recitation of market globalism's core claims and slogans have the capacity to produce what they name. As more neoliberal policies are enacted, the claims of market globalism become even more firmly planted in the public mind.

Analyzing hundreds of newspaper and magazine articles—both online and offline—I have identified five major ideological claims that occur with great regularity in the utterances, speeches, and writings of influential market globalists.

It is important to note that globalists themselves construct these ideological claims in order to sell their political and economic agenda. Perhaps no single market-globalist speech or piece of writing contains all of the five assertions discussed below, but all of them contain at least some of these claims.

· · · · ·

THE FIVE CLAIMS OF MARKET GLOBALISM

1. Claim 1: Globalization is about the liberalization and global integration of markets.

2. Claim 2: Globalization is inevitable and irreversible.

3. Claim 3: Nobody is in charge of globalization.

4. Claim 4: Globalization benefits everyone.

5. Claim 5: Globalization furthers the spread of democracy in the world.

· · · · ·

Like all ideologies, market globalism starts with the attempt to establish an authoritative definition of its core concepts. For neoliberals, such an account is anchored in the idea of the self-regulating market that serves as the framework for a future global order. As we noted in Chapter 3, neoliberals seek to cultivate in the popular mind the uncritical association of "globalization" with what they assert to be the benefits of market liberalization. In particular, they present the liberalization and integration of global markets as "natural" phenomena that further individual liberty and material progress in the world. Here are two examples of claim 1:

> Globalization is about the triumph of markets over governments. Both proponents and opponents of globalization agree that the driving force today is markets, which are suborning the role of government. (*Business Week*, December 13, 1999)

> One role [of government] is to get out of the way—to remove barriers to the free flow of goods, services, and capital. (Joan Spiro, former US undersecretary of state in the Clinton administration)

The problem with claim 1 is that its core message of liberalizing and integrating markets is only realizable through the *political* project of engineering free markets. Thus, market globalists must be prepared to utilize the *powers of government* to weaken and eliminate those social policies and institutions that curtail the market. Since only strong governments are up to this ambitious task of transforming existing social arrangements, the successful liberalization of markets depends upon *intervention* and *interference* by centralized state power. Such actions, however, stand in stark contrast to the neoliberal idealization of the limited role of government.

Yet, globalists do expect governments to play an extremely active role in implementing their political agenda. The activist character of neoliberal administrations in the United States, the United Kingdom, Australia, and New Zealand during the 1980s and 1990s attests to the importance of strong governmental action in engineering free markets.

Moreover, the claim that globalization is about the liberalization and global integration of markets solidifies as "fact" what is actually a contingent political initiative. Globalists have been successful because they have persuaded the public that their neoliberal account of globalization represents an objective, or at least a neutral, diagnosis of the very conditions it purports to analyze. To be sure, neoliberals may indeed be able to offer some "empirical evidence" for the "liberalization" of markets. But does the spread of market principles really happen because there exists a metaphysical connection between globalization and the expansion of markets? More likely, it occurs because globalists have the political and discursive power to shape the world largely according to their ideological formula:

Liberalization + Integration of Markets = Globalization

Claim 2 establishes the historical inevitability and irreversibility of globalization understood as the liberalization and global integration of markets. Let us consider the following statements:

> Today we must embrace the inexorable logic of globalization—
> that everything from the strength of our economy to the safety of
> our cities, to the health of our people, depends on events not only
> within our borders, but half a world away. . . . Globalization is
> irreversible. (Bill Clinton, former US president)

We need much more liberalization and deregulation of the Indian economy. No sensible Indian businessman disagrees with this. . . . Globalization is inevitable. There is no better alternative. (Rahul Bajaj, Indian industrialist)

The portrayal of globalization as some sort of natural force, like the weather or gravity, makes it easier for market globalists to convince people that they must adapt to the discipline of the market if they are to survive and prosper. Hence, the claim of inevitability depoliticizes the public discourse about globalization. Neoliberal policies are portrayed to be above politics; they simply carry out what is ordained by nature. This implies that, instead of acting according to a set of choices, people merely fulfill world-market laws that demand the elimination of government controls. As former British prime minister Margaret Thatcher used to say, "there is no alternative." If nothing can be done about the natural movement of

In this November 1, 1993, photograph, President Bill Clinton speaks to the Washington Chamber of Commerce in support of NAFTA.

economic and technological forces, then political groups ought to acquiesce and make the best of an unalterable situation. Resistance would be unnatural, irrational, and dangerous.

Market globalism's deterministic language offers yet another rhetorical advantage. If the natural laws of the market have indeed preordained a neoliberal course of history, then globalization does not reflect the arbitrary agenda of a particular social class or group. In that case, market globalists would merely carry out the imperatives of an unalterable force. People aren't in charge of globalization; markets and technology are. Here are two examples of claim 3:

> And the most basic truth about globalization is this: No one is in charge. . . . We all want to believe that someone is in charge and responsible. But the global marketplace today is an Electronic Herd of often anonymous stock, bond and currency traders and multinational investors, connected by screens and networks. (Thomas Friedman, *New York Times* correspondent and award-winning author)

> The great beauty of globalization is that no one is in control. The great beauty of globalization is that it is not controlled by any individual, any government, any institution. (Robert Hormats, vice chairman of Goldman Sachs International)

But Mr. Hormats is right only in a formal sense. While there is no conscious conspiracy orchestrated by a single, evil force, this does not mean that nobody is in charge of globalization. The liberalization and integration of global markets does not proceed outside the realm of human choice. As we will discuss in the final chapter, the

Robert Hormats, vice chairman of Goldman Sachs International, is shown here at the World Economic Forum in Davos, Switzerland, in 1996.

market-globalist initiative to integrate and deregulate markets around the world both creates and sustains asymmetrical power relations. The United States is by far the strongest economic and military power in the world, and the largest TNCs are based in North America. This is not to say that the "American Empire" rules supremely over these gigantic processes of globalization. But it *does* suggest that both the substance and the direction of globalization are to a significant degree shaped by American domestic and foreign policy.

Claim 4—globalization benefits everyone—lies at the very core of market globalism because it provides an affirmative answer to the crucial normative question of whether globalization should be considered a "good" or a "bad" thing. Market globalists frequently connect their arguments to the alleged benefits resulting from trade liberalization: rising global living standards, economic efficiency, individual freedom, and unprecedented technological progress. Let us consider the following two examples:

> There can be little doubt that the extraordinary changes in global finance on balance have been beneficial in facilitating significant improvements in economic structures and living standards throughout the world. (Alan Greenspan, former chairman of the US Federal Reserve Board)

> Globalization's effects have been overwhelmingly good. Spurred by unprecedented liberalization, world trade continues to expand faster than overall global economic output, inducing a wave of productivity and efficiency and creating millions of jobs. (Peter Sutherland, chairman of British Petroleum)

Mr. Sutherland does not seem to question the ideological assumptions behind his statement. Where are "millions of jobs" created?

Alan Greenspan, former chairman of the US Federal Reserve Board of Governors, spoke at the Per Jacobsson Foundation Lecture, part of the IMF Annual Meetings, October 21, 2007.

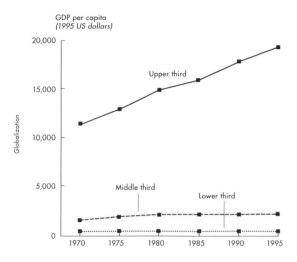

Diverging incomes of rich and poor countries, 1970–95.
Source: World Bank, *World Development Report 1999–2000.*

Who has benefited from globalization? When the market goes too far in dominating social and political outcomes, the opportunities and rewards of globalization are spread often unequally, concentrating power and wealth among a select group of people, regions, and corporations at the expense of the multitude.

China and India are often referred to as the great "winners" of globalization in the South. But their astonishing economic growth and the rise of per capita income comes disproportionately from the top 10 percent of the population. Indeed, the incomes of the bottom 50 percent in India and China have actually stagnated or even declined during the 2000s. Data provided by the World Bank suggest that income disparities between nations are widening at a quicker pace than ever before in recent history.

The low US unemployment rate in the 1990s is masked by low wages and millions of part-time laborers who are registered as employed but cannot get a full-time job. This photograph taken shortly before the US Congress's ratification of the North American Free Trade Agreement (NAFTA) shows farmers demonstrating in front of the Capitol Building in Washington, DC.

Data published in the 1999 and 2000 editions of the UN *Human Development Report* show that, before the onset of globalization in 1973, the income ratio between the richest and poorest countries was at about 44 to 1. Twenty-five years later it had climbed to 74 to 1. In the period since the end of the Cold War, the number of persons subsisting below

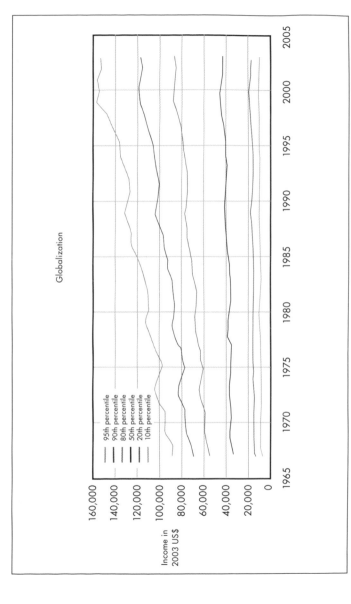

Household shares of aggregate income in the United States, 1967–2003.
Source: US Census Bureau, http://www.census.gov.

the international poverty line rose from 1.2 billion in 1987 to 1.5 billion today. If current trends persist, their numbers will reach 1.9 billion by 2015. This means that, at the dawn of the twenty-first century, the bottom 25 percent of humankind live on less than $140 a year. Meanwhile, the world's two hundred richest people have doubled their net worth to more than $1 trillion between 1994 and 1998. The assets of the world's top three billionaires are more than the combined GNP of all the least developed countries and their six hundred million people.

The same trend toward growing inequality can be observed even in the world's richest countries. Consider, for example, the widening income gap in the United States. At the same time, the number of political action committees in America increased from four hundred in 1974 to about nine thousand in 2000. Such corporate lobbyists successfully pressure Congress and the president to stay on a neoliberal course. Over one-third of the US workforce, 47 million workers, make less than ten dollars per hour and work 160 hours longer per year than did workers in 1973. The low US unemployment rate in the 1990s, often cited by globalists as evidence for the economic benefits of globalization, is masked by low wages and millions of part-time laborers who are registered as employed if they work as few as twenty-one hours a week and cannot get a full-time job. At the same time, the average salary of a CEO employed in a large corporation has risen dramatically. In 2000, it was 416 times higher than that of an average worker. The financial wealth of the top 1 percent of American households exceeds the combined wealth of the bottom 95 percent of households, reflecting a significant increase in the last twenty years.

There are numerous other indications confirming that the global hunt for profits actually makes it more difficult for poor people to enjoy the benefits of technology and scientific innovation. For example, there is widespread evidence for the existence of a widening "digital divide" separating countries in the global North and South.

Claim 5—globalization furthers the spread of democracy in the world—is rooted in the neoliberal assertion that free markets and democracy are synonymous terms. Persistently affirmed as "common sense," the actual compatibility of these concepts often goes unchallenged in the public discourse. Here are two examples:

> The level of economic development resulting from globalization is conducive to the creation of complex civil societies with a powerful middle class. It is this class and societal structure that facilitates democracy. (Francis Fukuyama, Johns Hopkins University)

> The Electronic Herd will intensify pressures for democratization generally, for three very critical reasons—flexibility, legitimacy, and sustainability. (Thomas Friedman, *New York Times* correspondent and award-winning author)

These arguments hinge on a conception of democracy that emphasizes formal procedures such as voting at the expense of the direct participation of broad majorities in political and economic decision making. This "thin" definition of democracy reflects an elitist and regimented model of "low-intensity" or "formal" market democracy. In practice, the crafting of a few democratic elements onto a basically authoritarian structure ensures that those elected remain insulated from popular pressures and thus can govern "effectively." Hence, the assertion that globalization furthers the spread of democracy in the world is largely based on a superficial definition of democracy.

Global Internet Users as a Percentage of the Regional Population

WORLD REGIONS	POPULATION (2007 EST.)	POPULATION % OF WORLD	INTERNET USAGE, LATEST DATA	% POPULATION (PENETRATION)	USAGE % OF WORLD	% USAGE GROWTH 2000–2007
Africa	941,249,130	14.2	44,361,940	4.7	3.4	882.7
Asia	3,733,783,474	56.5	510,478,743	13.7	38.7	346.6
Europe	801,821,187	12.1	348,125,847	43.4	26.4	231.2
Middle East	192,755,045	2.9	33,510,500	17.4	2.5	920.2
North America	334,659,631	5.1	238,015,529	71.1	18.0	120.2
Latin America / Caribbean	569,133,474	8.6	126,203,714	22.2	9.6	598.5
Oceania / Australia	33,569,718	0.5	19,175,836	57.1	1.5	151.6
WORLD TOTAL	6,606,971,659	100.0	1,319,872,109	20.0	100.0	265.6

Source: http://www.internetworldstats.com. © 2000–2008, Miniwatts Marketing Group. All rights reserved worldwide.

Notes: Internet Usage and World Population Statistics are for December 31, 2007. Demographic (population) numbers are based on data from the US Census Bureau. Internet usage information comes from data published by Nielsen/NetRatings, by the International Telecommunications Union, by local NIC, and other reliable sources.

Our examination of the five central claims of market globalism suggests that the neoliberal language about globalization is ideological in the sense that it is politically motivated and contributes toward the construction of particular meanings of globalization that preserve and stabilize existing power relations. But the ideological reach of market globalism goes far beyond the task of providing the public with a narrow explanation of the meaning of globalization. Market globalism consists of powerful narratives that sell an overarching neoliberal worldview, thereby creating collective meanings and shaping people's identities. Yet, as both the massive justice-globalist protests and the jihadist-globalist agenda in the 1990s and 2000s have shown, the expansion of market globalism has encountered considerable resistance.

Justice Globalism

As the twentieth century was drawing to a close, criticisms of market globalism began to receive more attention in the public discourse on globalization, a development aided by a heightened awareness of how extreme corporate profit strategies were leading to widening global disparities in wealth and well-being. Between 1999 and 2001, the contest between market globalism and its ideological challenger on the political Left erupted in street confrontations in many cities around the world. Who are these justice-globalist forces and what is their ideological vision?

Justice globalism refers to the political ideas and values associated with the social alliances and political actors increasingly known as the "social justice movement." It emerged in the 1990s as a progressive network of nongovernmental organizations that see themselves as a "global civil society" dedicated to the establishment of a more equitable relationship between the global North and South, the protection of the global environment, fair trade and international labor issues, human rights, and women's issues. Challenging the central claims of market globalism, justice globalists believe that "another world is possible," as one of their central slogans suggests. Envisioning the constructing of a new world order based on a global redistribution of wealth and power, justice globalists emphasize the crucial connection between globalization and local well-being. They accuse market-globalist elites of pushing neoliberal policies that are leading to greater global inequality, high levels of unemployment, environmental degradation, and the demise of social welfare. Calling for a "Global New Deal" favoring the marginalized and poor, justice globalists seek to protect ordinary people all over the world from a neoliberal "globalization from above."

In the United States, the consumer advocate Ralph Nader and the human rights proponent Noam Chomsky represent leading representatives of justice globalism. In Europe, the spokespersons for established Green parties have long suggested that unfettered neoliberal globalization has resulted in a serious degradation of the global environment. Neo-anarchist groups in Europe and the United States concur with this perspective, but, unlike the pacifist Greens, they are willing to make selective use of violent means in order to achieve their objectives. In the global South, justice globalism is represented by democratic-popular movements of resistance against neoliberal policies, such as the Zapatistas in Mexico, the Chipko movement in India, or local-global communitarians like the Filipino public intellectual Walden Bello. Most of these groups have forged close links to formidable justice-globalist INGOs.

Today, there exist thousands of these organizations in all parts of the world. Some consist only of a handful of activists, while others attract

Ralph Nader, shown speaking at an event in Portland, Oregon, in April 2004, while campaigning for his presidential bid, is a harsh critic of corporate globalization and the founder of several nonprofit organizations, including Global Trade Watch, the leading antiglobalist watchdog organization monitoring the activities of the IMF, WTO, and World Bank.

a much larger membership. For example, the Third World Network is a nonprofit international network of organizations based in Malaysia with regional offices on all five continents. Its objectives are to conduct research on development issues pertaining to the South and to provide a platform for justice-globalist perspectives at international meetings. The International Forum on Globalization is a global alliance of activists, scholars, economists, researchers, and writers formed to stimulate more effective responses to market globalism. Finally, transnational women's networks draw on women's groups from countries around the world to develop common policy initiatives, typically proposals pertaining to women's rights. Given the fact that many victims of neoliberal structural adjustment programs are women in the global South, it is not surprising to observe the rapid growth of these organizations.

In the 2000s, the forces of justice globalism have gathered political strength. This is evidenced by the emergence of the World Social Forum (WSF) as the key ideological site that draws to its annual meetings in Brazil or India tens of thousands of delegates from around the world. The proponents of justice globalism deliberately set up the WSF as a "shadow organization" to the market-globalist World Economic Forum (WEF) in Davos, Switzerland. Just like market globalists who treat the WEF as a platform to project their ideas and values to a global audience, justice globalists utilize the WSF as the main production site of their ideological and policy alternatives.

· · · · ·

FROM THE WSF CHARTER OF PRINCIPLES

1. The World Social Forum is an open meeting place for reflective thinking, democratic debate of ideas, formulation of proposals, free exchange of experiences, and interlinking for effective action by groups and movements of civil society that are opposed to neoliberalism and to domination of the world by capital and any form of imperialism and are committed to building a planetary society directed toward fruitful relationships among humankind and between it and the Earth. . . . 8. The World Social Forum is a plural, diversified, confessional, nongovernmental, and non-party context that, in a decentralized fashion, interrelates organizations and movements engaged in concrete action at levels from the local to the international to build another world. . . . 13. As a context for interrelations, the World Social Forum seeks to strengthen and create new national and international links among organizations and movement of society that—in both public and private life—will

increase the capacity for non-violent social resistance to the process of dehumanization the world is undergoing.

· · · · ·

Most of the justice-globalist groups affiliated with the WSF started out as small, seemingly insignificant groups of like-minded people. Many of them learned important theoretical and practical lessons from justice-globalist struggles in developing countries, particularly from Mexico's Zapatista rebellion. On January 1, 1994, the day NAFTA went into effect, a small band of indigenous rebels calling themselves the Zapatista Army of National Liberation captured four cities in the Chiapas region of southeast Mexico. Engaging in a number of skirmishes with the Mexican army and police over the next few years, the Zapatistas continued to protest the implementation of NAFTA and what their leader, Subcomandante Marcos, called the "global economic process to eliminate that multitude of people who are not useful to the powerful." In addition, the Zapatistas put forward a comprehensive program that pledged to reverse the destructive consequences of neoliberal free-market policies.

Many justice-globalist groups, which began as small, seemingly insignificant groups of like-minded people, learned important theoretical and practical lessons from justice-globalist struggles in developing countries, particularly from Mexico's Zapatista rebellion. This undated photograph shows Mexican revolutionary leader Emelio Zapata (1879–1919), from whom the modern-day Zapatistas took their inspiration.

Although the Zapatistas insisted that a major part of their struggle related to the restoration of the political and economic rights of indigenous peoples and the poor in Mexico, they also emphasized that the fight against neoliberalism had to be waged globally.

A clear indication of an impending large-scale confrontation between the forces of market globalism and its challengers on the Left came in November 1999, when forty thousand to fifty thousand people took part in the anti-WTO protests in Seattle. In spite of the predominance of North American participants, there was also a significant international presence. Activists like José Bové, a French sheep farmer who became an international celebrity for trashing a McDonald's outlet, marched shoulder to shoulder with Indian farmers and leaders of the Philippines' peasant movement. Articulating the main justice-globalist claims featured above, this eclectic alliance included consumer activists, labor activists (including students demonstrating against sweatshops), environmentalists, animal rights activists, advocates of Third World debt relief, feminists, and human rights proponents. Criticizing the WTO's neoliberal position on agriculture, multilateral investments, and intellectual property rights, this impressive crowd represented more than seven hundred organizations and groups.

On the opening day of the meeting, large groups of demonstrators interrupted traffic in the city center. They managed to block off the main entrances to the convention center by forming human chains. Many demonstrators who had been trained in nonviolent methods of resistance called for blocking key intersections and entrances in order to shut down the WTO meeting before it even started. As hundreds of delegates were scrambling to make their way to the conference center, Seattle police stepped up their efforts to clear the streets. Soon they launched

There was a significant international presence among the antiglobalization demonstrators at the WTO Ministerial Conference in Seattle, Washington. Among the international representatives was José Bové, who appears here in a 1999 photograph with the Space Needle in the background. Bové is a French sheep farmer and the leader of the French Farmers' Confederation, who first came to international notice when he led a group in the destruction of a McDonald's restaurant in France.

tear gas canisters into the crowds—including throngs of people who were peacefully sitting on streets and pavements. Having failed to accomplish their goal a few hours later, the Seattle police employed batons, rubber bullets, and pepper spray stingers against the remaining demonstrators. Some police officers even resorted to such methods as using their thumbs to grind pepper spray into the eyes of their victims and kicking nonviolent protesters in the groin. Altogether, the police arrested over six hundred persons. Significantly, the charges against over five hundred of them were eventually dismissed. Only fourteen cases actually went to trial, ultimately yielding ten plea bargains, two acquittals, and only two guilty verdicts.

November 30, 1999, in Seattle, Washington, police spray pepper spray to scatter the antiglobalization demonstrators protesting outside the meeting place of the WTO Ministerial Conference.

To be sure, there were perhaps two hundred individuals who, having declined to pledge themselves to nonviolent direct action, delighted in smashing storefronts and turning over garbage cans. Most of these youthful protesters belonged to the "Black Bloc," an Oregon-based anarchist organization ideologically opposed to free-market capitalism and centralized state power. Wearing dark hoods and black jackboots, Black Bloc members damaged stores that had been identified as engaging in extremely callous business practices. For example, they spared a Charles Schwab outlet, but smashed the windows of Fidelity Investments for maintaining high stakes in Occidental Petroleum, the oil company most responsible for violence against indigenous people in Colombia. They moved against Starbucks because of the company's nonsupport at the time of fair-traded coffee, but not against Tully's. They stayed away from REI stores, but inflicted damage on Gap outlets because of the company's heavy reliance on sweatshops in Asia.

Negotiations inside the conference center did not proceed smoothly either. Struggling to overcome the handicap of a late start, the WTO delegates soon deadlocked over such important issues as international labor and environmental standards. Many delegates from the global South refused to support an agenda that had been drafted by the major economic powers behind closed doors. Caught between two rebellions, one inside and one outside the conference center, officials sought to put a positive spin on the events. While emphasizing the alleged benefits of free trade and globalization, President Clinton nonetheless admitted that the WTO needed to implement "some internal reforms." In the end, the meeting in Seattle failed to produce substantive agreements.

Ironically, the Battle of Seattle proved that many of the new technologies hailed by globalists as the true hallmark of globalization could also be employed in the service of justice-globalist forces and their political agenda. For example, the Internet and text messaging have enabled the organizers of events like the one in Seattle to arrange for new forms of protest such as a series of demonstrations held simultaneously in various cities around the globe. Individuals and groups all over the world can utilize the Internet to readily and rapidly recruit new members, establish dates, share experiences, arrange logistics, identify and publicize targets—activities that only two decades ago would have demanded much more time and money. Other new technologies, like mobile phones, allow demonstrators not only to maintain close contact throughout the event, but also to react quickly and effectively to shifting police tactics. This enhanced ability to arrange and coordinate protests without the need of a central command, a clearly defined leadership, a large bureaucracy, and significant financial resources has added an entirely new dimension to the nature of street demonstrations.

In the months following the Battle of Seattle, justice-globalist demonstrations spiked around the world. For example, in Washington, DC, in April 2000, thirty thousand activists attempted to shut down the semiannual meetings of the IMF and the World Bank. In September, ten thousand protesters attempted to disrupt the annual meeting of the IMF and the World Bank in Prague. In January 2001, justice globalists descended on the World Economic Forum's annual meeting in the Swiss mountain resort of Davos. In what has been described as the country's largest security operation since the Second World War, thousands of police and military units engaged in street battles with demonstrators. In April, over thirty thousand justice-globalist protesters marched at the Summit of the Americas. Street confrontations erupted between police and some demonstrators. Two months later, thousands of demonstrators jammed London's main shopping area. But disciplined police units and nonviolent demonstrators managed to avoid serious clashes. In June, thousands of people demonstrated against market globalism at the European Union Summit in Gothenburg, Sweden. Peaceful marches turned violent and three protesters were shot with live ammunition. Finally, in July 2001, one hundred thousand justice-globalist demonstrators descended on the G8 Summit in Genoa, Italy. Protests turned violent when a small group of anarchists got into running battles with police. Dozens of people were injured, and one protester was shot dead by police.

To summarize, then, justice globalism entails both critical and constructive ideological claims. At the core of its extensive critique of the five claims of market globalism one can find counterclaims alleging that the liberalization and global integration of free markets leads to greater social inequalities, environmental destruction, the escalation of global conflicts and violence, the weakening of participatory forms of democracy, the proliferation of self-interest and consumerism, and the further marginalization of the powerless around the world. On the constructive side, justice globalism translates the global imaginary into a concrete political program reflected in the following nine demands:

1. A global "Marshall Plan" that includes a blanket forgiveness of all Third World debt.

2. Levying of the so-called Tobin Tax: a tax on international financial transactions that would benefit the global South.

3. Abolition of offshore financial centers that offer tax havens for wealthy individuals and corporations.

4. Implementation of stringent global environmental agreements.

5. Implementation of a more equitable global development agenda.

6. Establishment of a new world development institution financed largely by the global North through such measures as a financial transaction tax and administered largely by the global South.

7. Establishment of international labor protection standards, perhaps as clauses of a profoundly reformed WTO.

8. Greater transparency and accountability provided to citizens by national governments and international institutions.

9. Making all governance of globalization explicitly gender sensitive.

Jihadist Globalism

Justice globalists were preparing for a new wave of demonstrations against the IMF and World Bank, when, on September 11, 2001, three hijacked commercial airliners hit, in short succession, the World Trade Center in New York and the Department of Defense's Pentagon Building in Washington, DC. A fourth plane crashed in Pennsylvania before the hijackers were able to reach their intended target, most likely the White House. Nearly three thousand innocent people perished in less than two hours, including hundreds of heroic New York police and firefighters trapped in the collapsing towers of the World Trade Center. In the weeks following the attacks, it became clear that the operation had been planned and executed years in advance by the Al-Qaeda terrorist network.

As we noted in Chapter 1, religiously based organizations like bin Laden's Al-Qaeda terrorist network feed on the common perception not only that Western modes of modernization have failed to put an end to widespread poverty in the region, but that they have also enhanced political instability and strengthened secular tendencies in their own societies. Thus, jihadist globalism is a response to what is often experienced as a materialistic assault by the liberal or secular world. Drawing on revivalist themes popularized in the eighteenth century by theologian Muhammad ibn Abd al-Wahhab, bin Laden and his followers seek to globalize a "pure" and "authentic" form of Islam—by any means necessary. Their enemies are not merely the American-led forces of market globalism, but also those domestic groups who have accepted these alien influences and imposed them on Muslim peoples.

Osama bin Laden has left no doubt that the men linked to his organization committed the atrocities of 9/11 in response to the perceived "Americanization" of the world: the expansion of the American military around the globe, especially the presence of US military bases in Saudi Arabia; the internationalization of the 1991 Gulf War; the escalation of the Palestinian-Israeli conflict; the "paganism," "secularism," and "materialism" of American-led market globalism; and the eighty-year history of "humiliation and disgrace" perpetrated against the global *umma* (Islamic community of believers) by a sinister global "Judeo-Crusader alliance."

This photograph shows the South Tower of the World Trade Center bursting into flames after being struck by hijacked United Airlines Flight 175.

Clearly, it would be a mistake to equate jihadist globalism of the Al-Qaeda variety with the religion of Islam or even more peaceful strands of "political Islam" or "Islamist fundamentalism." Rather, the term "jihadist globalism" is meant to apply to those extremely violent strains of religiously influenced ideologies that articulate the global imaginary into concrete political agendas and terrorist strategies. Thus, in principle, the label "jihadist globalism" applies also to the ideology of those violent fundamentalists in the West who seek to turn the whole world into a "Christian empire." At the same time, however, it must be emphasized that jihadist globalism Al-Qaeda-style is the most influential and successful attempt yet to articulate the rising global imaginary around the core concepts of *umma* and *jihad* (armed or unarmed struggle against unbelief purely for the sake of God and his *umma*).

Indeed, bin Laden understands the *umma* as a single community of believers united in their belief in the one and only God. Expressing a populist yearning for strong leaders who set things right by fighting alien invaders and corrupt Islamic elites, he and his followers claim to return power back to the "Muslim masses" and restore the *umma* to its earlier glory. In their view, the process of regeneration must start with a small but dedicated vanguard willing to sacrifice their lives as martyrs to the holy cause of awakening people to their religious duties—not just in traditionally Islamic countries, but wherever members of the *umma* yearn for the establishment of God's rule on earth. With a third of the world's Muslims living today as minorities in non-Islamic countries, bin Laden regards the restoration as no longer a local, national, or even regional event. Rather, it requires a concerted *global* effort spearheaded by jihadists operating in various localities around the world.

Thus, Al-Qaeda's desired Islamization of modernity takes place in a global space emancipated from the confining territoriality of "Egypt," or the "Middle East" that used to constitute the political framework of religious nationalists fighting modern secular regimes in the twentieth century. Although Al-Qaeda embraces the dualism of a "clash of civilizations" between its imagined *umma* and "global unbelief," its globalist ideology clearly transcends clear-cut civilizational fault lines. Its desire for the restoration of a transnational *umma* attests to the globalization of the Muslim world just as much as it reflects the Islamization of the West. Constructed in the ideational transition from the national to the global imaginary, jihadist globalism still retains potent metaphors that resonate with people's national or even tribal solidarities. And yet, Al-Qaeda's focus is firmly on the global as its leaders have successfully redirected militant Islamism's struggle from the traditional "Near Enemy" (secular-nationalist Middle Eastern regimes) to the "Far Enemy" (the globalizing West).

Al-Qaeda's core ideological claim—to rebuild a unified global *umma* through global jihad against global unbelief—resonates well with the dynamics of a globalizing world. It holds special appeal for Muslim youths between the ages of fifteen and thirty who have lived for sustained periods of time in the individualized and decultured environments of Westernized Islam. This "second wave" of jihadist recruits, responsible for the most spectacular terrorist operations between 9/11 and the London bombings of 7/7 (2005), are products of a Westernized Islam. Most of them resided in Europe or North Africa and had few or no links to traditional Middle East political parties. Their enthusiasm for the establishment of a transnational *umma* by means of jihad and Al-Qaeda's rigid religious code, divorced from

American Airlines # 11

Al Suqami   Waleed M. Alshehri   Wail M. Alshehri   Alomari   Atta

In the view of bin Laden and his followers, the process of returning power back to the "Muslim masses" and restoring the *umma* to its earlier glory must start with a small but dedicated vanguard willing to sacrifice their lives as martyrs to the holy cause, exemplified by the men responsible for the terrorists attacks of 9/11 and 7/7. This composite of mug shots shows (left to right) Satam Al Suqami, Waleed M. Alshehri, Wail Alshehri, Abdulaziz Alomari, and Mohamed Atta, the men suspected of hijacking American Airlines Flight 11 and flying it into the World Trade Center.

traditional cultural contexts, made them prime candidates for recruitment. These young men followed in the footsteps of Al-Qaeda's "first-wavers" in Afghanistan in the 1980s who developed their ideological outlook among a multinational band of idealistic mujahideen bent on bringing down the "godless" Soviet Empire.

If the restored, purified *umma*—imagined to exist in global space that transcends particular national and tribal identities—is the final goal of jihadist globalism, then jihad surely serves as its principal means. For our purposes, it is not necessary to reproduce the long scholastic debates about the many meanings and "correct" applications of *jihad*. It suffices to note that jihadist globalists like bin Laden and his deputy Ayman al-Zawahiri endorse both "offensive" and "defensive" versions of jihad. They celebrate jihad as the "peak" or "pinnacle" of Islam, emphasizing that armed struggle against global unbelief is obligatory on the entire *umma*. For Al-Qaeda, jihad represents the sole path toward the noble goal of creating a global *umma* based on "correct beliefs" because their *da'wa* (preaching; admonishing) has failed to reform the treacherous Muslim elites or convert the hostile "crusaders." And since 9/11, at the latest, the world knows that jihadist globalists are not choosy about the kind of jihad they have in mind: any form of struggle that might weaken the enemy. Such tactics include large-scale terrorist attacks, suicide bombings, and public killings of hostages.

Their extremist rhetoric notwithstanding, bin Laden and his sympathizers never lose sight of the fact that jihadist globalists are fighting a steep uphill battle against the forces of market globalism. For example, in his videotaped message of September 6, 2007, he discussed in much detail the ability of "American media imperialism" to "seduce the Muslim world" with its consumerist message. He also makes frequent references to a "continuing and biased campaign" waged against jihadist globalism by the corporate media—"especially Hollywood"—for the purpose of misrepresenting Islam and hiding the "failures of the Western democratic system." He repeatedly accuses the United States of trying to change the region's ideology through the imposition of Western-style democracy and the "Americanization of our culture."

· · · · ·

OSAMA BIN LADEN ON JIHAD AND AMERICA

And the West's notion that Islam is a religion of *jihad* and enmity toward the religions of the infidels and the infidels themselves is an accurate and true depiction. . . . For it is, in fact, part of our religion to impose our particular beliefs on others. . . . Their [moderate Muslims] reluctance in acknowledging that Offensive *Jihad* is one of the exclusive traits of our religion demonstrates nothing but defeat.

(2003)

For example, Al-Qaeda spent $500,000 on the September 11 attacks, while America lost more than $500 billion, at the lowest estimate, in the event and its aftermath. That makes a million American dollars for every Al-Qaeda dollar, by the grace of God Almighty. This is in addition to the fact that it lost an enormous number of jobs—and for the federal deficit, it made record losses, estimated at over a trillion dollars.

Still more serious for America was the fact that the *mujahideen* forced Bush to resort to an emergency budget in order to continue fighting in Afghanistan and Iraq. This shows the success of our plan to bleed America to the point of bankruptcy, with Godís will.

(2004)

I tell you [Americans] that the war [on terror] will be either ours or yours. If it is the former, it will mean your loss and your shame forever—and the winds are blowing in this direction, by Allah's grace. But if it is the latter, then read history, for we are a people who do not stand for injustice, and we strive for vengeance all days of our lives. And the days and nights will not pass until we avenge ourselves as we did on September 11.

(2006)

. . . . .

And yet, even against seemingly overwhelming odds, Al-Qaeda leaders express their confidence in the ultimate triumph of jihad over "American Empire." Indeed, despite its chilling and violent content, bin Laden's vision contains an ideological alternative to both market globalism and justice globalism that nonetheless imagines community in unambiguously global terms.

EIGHT

Assessing the Future of Globalization

●

NO DOUBT, 9/11 AND THE ENSUING "global war on terror" gave an unexpected jolt to the struggle over the meaning and the direction of globalization. As George W. Bush made clear time and again, this new war was bound to be a lengthy conflict of global proportions. Throughout his second term in office, with Iraq still not pacified, the US president continued to appeal to a global audience to support America in what he called "the decisive military and ideological struggle of the twenty-first century."

This raises the final question we will consider in our examination of globalization: will the global fight against terrorism lead to more extensive forms of international cooperation and interdependence, or might it stop

While the powerful governments of the global North that dominate the WTO have been meeting to address the grave concerns of representatives from the global South about some of their policies, the powers of the global North have made it clear that they consider existing arrangements legally binding. This photograph, taken on July 28, 2008, shows the figure of Justice outside the WTO headquarters in Geneva, Switzerland.

the powerful momentum of globalization? On first thought, it seems highly implausible that even a protracted global war on terror could stop, or even slow down, such a powerful set of social processes as globalization. Yet, there are already some early warning signs. The implementation of more intense border controls and stringent security measures at the world's major air- and seaports have made travel and international trade more cumbersome. Calls for tightening national borders and maintaining sharp cultural divisions can be heard more frequently in public discourse. Belligerent patriotic sentiments are on display all over the world. Political leaders around the world—especially those whose democratic credentials are not exactly evident—are utilizing the "terrorism" label to stigmatize and marginalize their opponents.

A close look at modern history reveals that large-scale violent confrontations were capable of stopping and even reversing previous globalization trends. As we noted in Chapter 2, the period from 1860 to 1914 constituted an earlier phase of globalization, characterized by the expansion of transportation and communication networks, the rapid growth of international trade, and a huge flow of capital. Great Britain, then the most dominant of the world's "Great Powers," sought to spread its political system and cultural values across the globe much in the same way the United States does today. But this earlier period of globalization was openly imperialistic in character, involving the transfer of resources from the colonized global South in exchange for European manufactures. Liberalism, Great Britain's chief ideology, translated a national, not a global, imaginary into concrete political programs. In the end, these sustained efforts to engineer an "inter-national" market under the auspices of the British Empire resulted in a severe backlash that culminated in the outbreak of the Great War in 1914.

In an enduring study on this subject, the late political economist Karl Polanyi locates the origins of the social crises that gripped the world during the first half of the twentieth century in ill-conceived efforts to liberalize and globalize markets. Commercial interests came to dominate society by means of a ruthless market logic that effectively disconnected people's economic activities from their social relations. The competitive rules of the free market destroyed complex social relations of mutual obligation and undermined deep-seated norms and values such as civic engagement, reciprocity, and redistribution. As large segments of the population found themselves without an adequate system of social security and communal support, they resorted to radical measures to protect themselves against market globalization.

Polanyi notes that these European movements against unfettered capitalism eventually gave birth to political parties that forced the passage of protective social legislation on the national level. After a prolonged period of severe economic dislocation following the end of the Great War, such national-protectionist impulses experienced their most extreme manifestations in Italian fascism and German Nazism. In the end, the liberal dream of subordinating all nation-states to the requirements of the free market had generated an equally extreme countermovement that turned markets into mere appendices of the totalitarian state.

The applicability of Polanyi's analysis to the current situation seems obvious. Like its nineteenth-century predecessor, today's version of market globalism also represents a gigantic experiment in unleashing economic deregulation and a culture of consumerism on the entire world. Like nineteenth-century Britain, the United States draws both admiration and contempt from regions in the world that feel themselves to be oppressed and exploited by a global logic of economic integration led by a haughty "American Empire."

Strictly speaking, of course, the United States does not constitute an "empire." But one could make a reasonable case for the persistence of American imperialism as a continuous and largely informal process that started with the seventeenth-century expansionist settlement of the North American continent and periodically assumed more coercive expressions such as the annexation of the Hawaiian Islands, parts of Samoa, the Philippines, and Puerto Rico in the 1890s. More than a century later, however, the United States no longer exerts direct dominion or formal rule—the hallmark of any "empire"—over conquered people under its sovereign authority. And yet, the country has emerged from the Cold War as a new kind of empire of vast wealth, peerless military power, and global cultural reach. No doubt, America has become a "hyperpower" that considers the entire world its geopolitical sphere of influence.

After 9/11, it found itself in the historically unprecedented position of enforcing its own idea of global order—even in unilateral fashion if it so desired. Neoconservative American foreign policy experts began to express such sentiments when they argued that only a muscular United States willing to accept its imperial status was up to the task of stabilizing a world unsettled by the actions of jihadist globalists eager to get their hands on weapons of mass destruction. For such "hawks," the new environment of global insecurity presented nothing less than a clear-cut "case of American Empire." "Imperial globalism" might, therefore, be an apt characterization of this neoconservative inclination to shape the globe in the American image by military means. Its militaristic inclinations notwithstanding, the Bush administration constructed its imperial globalism within the established framework of market globalism. Although its new *National Security*

Strategy of the United States (2002; revised 2006) contains the famous preemption clause—the US government reserving the right to strike presumed "enemies" before they attack America—the document reaffirms unequivocally that worldwide establishment of free markets and free trade are the "key priorities" of American national security.

Thus, American empire and globalization are not necessarily opposites. Imperial globalism keeps all the major claims of market globalism with two important modifications. Claim 3, nobody is in charge of globalization, has been altered by open declarations on the part of the Bush administration that America stands ready to globally enforce the allegedly self-regulating market order. As a result, a new claim has been added to market globalism: globalization (understood as the liberalization and global integration of markets) requires a global war on terror.

But as we have seen in the previous chapter, the pronouncements of imperial globalism have not gone unchallenged. It is quite conceivable that the Al-Qaeda attacks of the last years were only the opening salvos of a widening global war waged by the US government and its allies against a growing list of terrorist organizations and their supporters around the world. The escalation of such a grim backlash scenario might well put the brakes on globalization.

On the other hand, it is also possible that the ongoing efforts to contain these violent forces of jihadist globalism might actually increase international cooperation and encourage the forging of new global alliances. In order to eradicate the social causes of terrorism, the global North might be willing to replace the dominant neoliberal version of globalization with a substantive reform agenda designed to reduce the existing disparities in global wealth and well-being. Unfortunately, despite their encouraging reassurances to put a "human face" on their predatory

To eradicate the primary social causes of terrorism, the global North has indicated that it might be willing to replace its dominant neoliberal agenda with a reform agenda aimed toward reducing the existing disparities in global wealth and well-being. English painter William Powell Frith (1819–1909) depicted the disparity between the wealthy and the impoverished in this painting created in 1888.

version of globalization, many market globalists have remained within the parameters of their corporate agenda. If implemented at all, their proposed "reforms" have remained largely symbolic in character.

For example, in the wake of the justice-globalist demonstrations, representatives of the wealthy countries joined the WTO secretary-general in assuring audiences worldwide that they would be willing to reform the economic institution's rules and structure in the direction of greater transparency and accountability. Yet, several years later, no concrete steps have been taken to honor these commitments. Granted, the WTO has been holding special General Council sessions to comply with the urgent requests of developing countries to review several of its questionable procedures. Yet, the spokespersons of the powerful governments in the global North that dominate the WTO have made it clear that they consider existing arrangements as legally binding. In their view, procedural problems can only be addressed in the context of a new, comprehensive round of multilateral negotiations conducted according to the very rules that are being contested by many developing countries and justice-globalist NGOs.

This strategy of fortifying the market-globalist paradigm with a new rhetoric of mild reformism might work for a relatively short period. But in the long run, the growth of global inequality and the persistence of social instability harbor the potential to unleash reactionary social forces that dwarf even those responsible for the suffering of millions during the 1930s and 1940s. Indeed, as recent developments have shown, globalization's very survival will depend on humanity's ability to tackle the three major global issues confronting us in the twenty-first century: global climate change, increasing economic inequality, and escalating political and social violence. In order to prevent a further escalation of the violent confrontation between market globalism and its ideological opponents, world leaders must design and implement a comprehensive Global New Deal that builds and extends genuine networks of solidarity around the world.

Without question, the years and decades ahead will bring further challenges. Humanity has reached yet another critical juncture. Lest we are willing to let global problems fester to the point where violence and intolerance appear to be the only realistic ways of confronting our unevenly integrating world, we must link the future course of globalization to a profoundly reformist agenda. As I have emphasized in the Preface of this book, there is nothing wrong with greater manifestations of social interdependence that emerge as a result of globalization. However, these transformative social processes must have a moral compass and an ethical polestar that guide our collective efforts: the building of a truly democratic and egalitarian global order that protects universal human rights without destroying the cultural diversity that is the lifeblood of human evolution.

REFERENCES

•

There is a great deal of academic literature on globalization, but many of these books are not easily accessible to those who are just setting out to acquire some knowledge of the subject. However, readers who have already digested the present volume may find it easier to approach some of the academic works listed below. While these books do not exhaust the long list of publications on the subject, they nonetheless represent what I consider to be the most appropriate sources for further reading. Indeed, some of them have influenced the arguments made in the present volume. Following the overall organization of the Brief Insights series, however, I have kept direct quotations to a minimum. Still, I wish to acknowledge my intellectual debt to the authors below, whose influence on this book is not always obvious from the text.

CHAPTER 1
Accessible academic books on globalization published in this decade include: James H. Mittelman, *The Globalization Syndrome* (Princeton University Press, 2000); Malcolm Waters, *Globalization*, 2nd ed. (Routledge, 2001); Jan Aart Scholte, *Globalization*, 2nd ed. (St. Martin's Press, 2005); David Held and Anthony McGrew, *Globalization/Anti-Globalization*, 2nd ed. (Polity, 2007); and Saskia Sassen, *A Sociology of Globalization* (Norton, 2007).

For representative collections of influential essays and excerpts on globalization, see George Ritzer (ed.), *The Blackwell Companion to Globalization* (Blackwell, 2007); and Frank J. Lechner and John Boli (eds.), *The Globalization Reader*, 3rd ed. (Wiley Blackwell, 2007). Even a decade after its publication, Manuel Castells's classic three-volume set, *The Information Age* (Blackwell, 1996–8), remains a comprehensive attempt to map the contours of the global information age. David Held and Anthony McGrew's anthology, *Globalization Theory* (Polity, 2007), also provides a clear elucidation of leading theoretical approaches to understanding globalization. Finally, Paul W. James's magisterial *Globalism,*

Nationalism, Tribalism: Bringing Theory Back In (Sage, 2006) illuminates the contradictions and unevenness of current globalization processes.

There are now several excellent academic journals dedicated to the study of globalization. The most influential are: *Globalizations*, *Global Networks*, and *New Global Studies*.

More information on the nature and role of the commercial enterprises mentioned in the chapter can be found on the Internet: http://www.english.aljazeera.net; http://www.timex.com.; http://www.kalashnikov.guns.ru.

The parable of the blind scholars and the elephant most likely originated in the Pali Buddhist Udana, a collection of Buddhist stories compiled in the second century BCE. The many versions of the parable spread to other religions as well, especially to Hinduism and Islam. I want to thank Professor Ramdas Lamb from the University of Hawaii for his explanations of the story.

CHAPTER 2

My discussion in the early part of this chapter has greatly benefited from the arguments made by Jared Diamond in his Pulitzer Prize–winning book, *Guns, Germs, and Steel* (Norton, 1999). I also recommend the delightful and very readable histories of globalization assembled by Nayan Chandra, *Bound Together: How Traders, Preachers, Adventurers, and Warriors Shaped Globalization* (Yale University Press, 2007); and Alex MacGillivray, *A Brief History of Globalization: The Untold Story of our Incredible Shrinking Planet* (Running Press, 2006).

Some of the essential books surveying the growing field of global history include: A. G. Hopkins (ed.), *Globalization in World History* (Norton, 2002) and *Global History* (Palgrave, 2006); Robbie Robertson, *Three Waves of Globalization* (Zed Books, 2004); Juergen Osterhammel and Niels P. Petersson, *Globalization: A Short History* (Princeton University Press, 2005); and Barry Gills and William Thompson (eds.), *Globalization and Global History* (Routledge, 2006). Two excellent academic journals on the subject are: *Journal of World History* and *Journal of Global History*.

The classic account of "world-system theory" is Immanuel Wallerstein, *The Capitalist World Economy* (Cambridge University Press, 1979). A powerful critique of its alleged Eurocentrism is contained in Andre Gunder Frank, *ReORIENT: Global Economy in the Asian Age* (University of California Press, 1998).

CHAPTER 3

Short, accessible introductions to economic globalization include Wayne Ellwood, *The No-Nonsense Guide to Globalization* (New Internationalist Publications, 2006); and Sarah Anderson and John Cavanagh with Thea Lee, *Field Guide to the Global Economy* (The New Press, 2005). More academic accounts include Dani Rodrik, *One Economics, Many Recipes: Globalization, Institutions, and Economic Growth* (Princeton University Press, 2007); Jeffry A. Frieden, *Global Capitalism: Its Fall and Rise in the Twentieth*

Century (Norton, 2007); Robert Gilpin, *Global Political Economy* (Princeton University Press, 2003); and Ankie Hoogvelt, *Globalization and the Postcolonial World* (Johns Hopkins University Press, 2001).

For the study of "networks" in our age of globalization, see Robert J. Holton, *Global Networks* (Palgrave Macmillan, 2008); and Manuel Castells, *The Internet Galaxy* (Oxford University Press, 2001).

The best sources for data on economic globalization are the annual editions of the UN *Human Development Report* (Oxford University Press) and the World Bank's *World Development Report* (Oxford University Press).

CHAPTER 4

David Held's seven points describing the Westphalian model can be found in David Held, Anthony McGrew, David Goldblatt, and Jonathan Perraton, *Global Transformations* (Stanford University Press, 1999), pp. 37–38. My own discussion of political globalization has greatly benefited from insights contained in Chapter 1 of this study. Another excellent introduction to political globalization is John Baylis and Steve Smith, *The Globalization of World Politics*, 4th ed. (Oxford University Press, 2008).

For the arguments of hyperglobalizers, see Martin Wolf, *Why Globalization Works* (Yale University Press, 2005); Lowell Bryan and Diana Farrell, *Market Unbound* (John Wiley & Sons, 1996); and Kenichi Ohmae, *The End of the Nation-State* (The Free Press, 1995) and *The Borderless World* (Harper Business, 1990).

For the arguments of the globalization skeptics, see John Ralston Saul, *The Collapse of Globalism* (Viking, 2005); Michel Chossudovsky, *The Globalization of Poverty and the New World Order* (Global Research, 2003); Peter Gowan, *The Global Gamble* (Verso, 1999); and Linda Weiss, *The Myth of the Powerless State* (Cornell University Press, 1998). Saskia Sassen's important work on territoriality and global cities contains both skeptical and hyperglobalist arguments. See, for example, *Territory, Authority, Rights: From Medieval to Global Assemblages* (Princeton University Press, 2008), and *The Global City: New York, London, Tokyo* (Princeton University Press, 2001).

On the topic of global politics, economics, and governance, see Heikki Patomaki, *The Political Economy of Global Security: War, Future Crises, and Changes in Global Governance* (Routledge, 2007); Friedrich V. Kratochwil and Edward D. Mansfield (eds.), *International Organization and Global Governance: A Reader* (Longman, 2005); Vincent Cable, *Globalization and Global Governance* (The Royal Institute of International Affairs, 1999); and Raimo Väyrynen, *Globalization and Global Governance* (Rowman & Littlefield, 1999). David Held's elements of cosmopolitan democracy are taken from Daniele Archibugi and David Held (eds.), *Cosmopolitan Democracy* (Polity Press, 1995), pp. 96–120.

CHAPTER 5

For two comprehensive studies on the cultural dimensions of globalization, see Jan Nederveen Pieterse, *Globalization and Culture: Global Melange* (Rowman and Littlefield, 2008); and John Tomlinson, *Globalization and Culture* (University of Chicago Press, 1999).

For the arguments of pessimistic hyperglobalizers, see Benjamin Barber, *Consumed* (W. W. Norton and Company, 2007); Serge Latouche, *The Westernization of the World* (Polity Press, 1996); and George Ritzer, *The McDonaldization of Society* (Pine Forge Press, 1993).

For the arguments of optimistic hyperglobalizers, Thomas L. Friedman, *The World Is Flat 3.0: A Brief History of the Twenty-First Century* (Picador, 2007) and Tyler Cowen, *Creative Construction: How Globalization Is Changing the World's Cultures* (Princeton University Press, 2004).

For the arguments of the skeptics, see Arjun Appadurai, *Modernity At Large* (University of Minnesota Press, 1996); Ulf Hannerz, *Transnational Connections* (Routledge, 1996); and Roland Robertson, *Globalization* (Sage, 1992).

For the role of the media, see Terry Flew, *Understanding Global Media* (Palgrave MacMillan, 2007); James D. White, *Global Media: Television Revolution in Asia* (Routledge, 2005); Lee Artz and Yahya R. Kamalipour (eds.), *The Globalization of Corporate Media Hegemony* (State University of New York Press, 2003); and Robert W. McChesney and Edward S.Herman, *The Global Media: Missionaries of Global Capitalism* (Cassell, 1998).

The figures on TV advertising are taken from Television Bureau of Advertising, "Advertising Volume in the United States," http://www. tvb.org; and Mass Media News, "Two TV Networks Running 15 Minutes of Ads," http://www.taa.winona.msus.edu/mediaupdate/00/ 11nov.html.

Accessible introductions to globalization and the environment include Hilary French, *Vanishing Borders* (W. W. Norton, 2000); and Chapter 8, "Catastrophe in the Making: Globalization and the Environment" in Held et al., *Global Transformations.*

CHAPTER 6

For the most comprehensive and up-to-date collection of data on global climate change, see S. George Philander, *Encyclopedia of Global Warming and Climate Change* (Sage, 2008). Accessible books on the subject include: Mark Lynas, *Six Degrees: Our Future on A Hotter Planet* (National Geographic, 2008); and Al Gore, *An Inconvenient Truth: The Crisis of Global Warming* (Viking, 2007).

For more general books on the ecological dimensions of globalization, see Jared Diamond, *Collapse: How Societies Choose to Fail or Succeed* (Penguin, 2005); and Franz Broswimmer, *Ecocide* (London: Pluto Press, 2002).

For the Stern Report, see Nicholas Stern, *The Economics of Climate Change: The Stern Review* (Cambridge University Press, 2007).

For an excellent summary of recent environmental summits and various environmental policy positions, see Peter Christoff, "The Bali Roadmap and Beyond," in *Arena Magazine* Vol. 93(2) 2008, pp. 32–39.

CHAPTER 7

For a more detailed account of the ideological dimensions of globalization, see Manfred B. Steger, *The Rise of the Global Imaginary: Political Ideologies from the French Revolution to the Global War on Terror* (Oxford University Press, 2008); and *Globalisms: The Great Ideological Struggle of the 21st Century* (Rowman & Littlefield, 2009).

Readable accounts of globalization from a market-globalist perspective include: Jagdish Bhagwati, *In Defense of Globalization* (Oxford University Press, 2007); Daniel Cohen, *Globalization and Its Enemies* (MIT Press, 2007); and Jeffrey E. Garten, *The Mind of the CEO* (Perseus Publishing, 2002).

Justice-globalist arguments and information on the WSF and the global justice movement can be found in: Jackie Smith and Marina Karides, *Global Democracy in the World Social Forums* (Paradigm, 2007); Donatella Della Porta, *The Global Justice Movement: Cross-National and Transnational Perspectives* (Paradigm, 2007); and Boaventura de Sousa Santos, *The Rise of the Global Left: The World Social Forum and Beyond* (Zed Books, 2006); John Cavanagh and Jerry Mander, *Alternatives to Economic Globalization: A Better World Is Possible* (Berrett-Koehler, 2004).

Two excellent academic treatments of jihadist globalism and its affiliated movements can be found in: Olivier Roy, *Globalized Islam: The Search for the New Ummah* (Columbia University Press, 2006); and Fawaz A. Gerges, *The Far Enemy: Why Jihad Went Global* (Cambridge University Press, 2005).

The excerpts from Osama bin Laden's speeches and writings are taken from Raymond Ibrahim (ed.), *The Al-Qaeda Reader* (Broadway Books, 2007); and Bruce Lawrence (ed.), *Messages to the World: The Statements of Osama bin Laden* (Verso 2005).

CHAPTER 8

For the discussion of the backlash against globalization in the interwar period, see Karl Polanyi, *The Great Transformation* (Beacon Press, 2001 [1944]).

There has been a proliferation of literature on globalization and American empire. Excellent treatments of the subject can be found in Chalmers Johnson, *Nemesis: The Last Days of the American Republic* (Holt, 2008); Jan Nederveen Pieterse, *Globalization or Empire?* (Routledge, 2004); and Neil Smith, *The Endgame of Globalization* (Routledge, 2004).

The National Security Strategy of the United States can be accessed online at: http://www.whitehouse.gov/ncs/nss.html.

INDEX

•

Page numbers in *italics* include illustrations and photographs/captions.

OECD (Organization for Economic Cooperation and Development), 84, 111
Ottoman Empire, 29

patriarchal societies, 27
Pepsi headquarters, *63*
planetarity aspects of globalization, 10
Polanyi, Karl, 163
politics
    centralization of, 76
    in China, 35
    core of, 14
    global governance and, 82–87, *86*
    global imaginary and, 12
    globality and, 9–10
    Green parties in, 142
    market globalism and, 129–30
    modern nation-states and, 75–79
    of nation-state, 78–82
population growth, 25–27, *106*–7, 109
poverty, 56, *58–59*, 118, *135*–38, *137*, *166*
preemptive military strikes, 164–65
protests, *122*–23, *146–48*, 150, 166

Reagan, Ronald, *54*, 55
Reformation, 35, 75
religion, 2, 9, 33, 35, 108, 152–55, 157–58
Ricardo, David, 52, *53*
Ridge, Tom, *81*
Ritzer, George, 92
Robertson, Roland, 15, 95
Roman Empire, 29, 31

Schuman, Robert, 84
self-determination, 75, 76–*77*, 126
shopping mall in Jakarta, Indonesia, *16–17*
Silk Road, *20*–21, 31

Smith, Adam, 52, *53*
social dimensions
    classes and, *27*, 35
    core, 14–18
    creation/multiplication aspects of, 14–16
    differing views of, 12–14
    expansion/stretching aspects of, *16–17*
    globality and, 9
    intensification/acceleration aspects of, 15, 17–18, 73, 89
    processes of, 10–12
social justice movement, 141
Southeast Asia financial crisis, 60–61
Soviet Union, 6–7, 46, 55, 67, 84
Spencer, Herbert, 53
Stern, Nicholas, 119
"Stern Report," 113–14, 117, 121
stock exchanges, 59–60
structural adjustment programs, 68–70
Summit of the Americas, 150
Sutherland, Peter, 134

taxes, 52, 56, 80, 151
technology. *See also* Internet
    Al-Jazeera network and, 3–6, 14–16
    Al-Qaeda using communications, 3, *4*
    in China, *30*–31
    influencing globalization, 21–22
    information/communications, 40–43, *42*, 97–98
    migration of, 34–35
    during modern period, 40
    political globalization and, 78–79
    speed of, 5, 17
    using satellites, *xii*–1, 17, 57
    wheel invention and, 28
    writing invention and, 28, *29*
telegraph, 40–*42*
territoriality, 74, 75, 79
terrorism, *81*, 152–59, *153*, *156*. *See also* Al-Qaeda; bin Laden, Osama

PICTURE CREDITS

•